Once Upon a Rhyme

Staffordshire

Edited by Donna Samworth

First published in Great Britain in 2011 by:

Young**Writers**

Young Writers
Remus House
Coltsfoot Drive
Peterborough
PE2 9BF
Telephone: 01733 890066
Website: www.youngwriters.co.uk

All Rights Reserved
Book Design by Tim Christian
© Copyright Contributors 2011
SB ISBN 978-0-85739-479-8

THIS BOOK BELONGS TO

....

Foreword

Here at Young Writers our objective is to help children discover the joys of poetry and creative writing. Few things are more encouraging for the aspiring writer than seeing their own work in print. We are proud that our anthologies are able to give young authors this unique sense of confidence and pride in their abilities.

Once Upon A Rhyme is our latest fantastic competition, specifically designed to encourage the writing skills of primary school children through the medium of poetry. From the high quality of entries received, it is clear that Once Upon A Rhyme really captured the imagination of all involved.

The resulting collection is an excellent showcase for the poetic talents of the younger generation and we are sure you will be charmed and inspired by it, both now and in the future.

Contents

Maddie Stewart is our featured poet this year. She has written a nonsense workshop for you and included some of her great poems. You can find these at the end of your book

Birchwood Primary School
Jessica Cole (9)	1
Jake Calcott (7)	1
William Ryan Gallett (8)	2
Pippa Randall (7)	2
Tabatha Carter (10)	3
Jamie Smart (7)	3
Kelsey Anne Cunningham (8)	4
Billy Randall (7)	4
Isobel Wilson (9)	5
Shannon White (7)	5
Chloe Bagshaw (11)	6
Harriett Steele (7)	6
Darcie Buchan (10)	7
Lewis James Bell (8)	7
Laura Doak (8)	8
Stephanie Manton (10)	8
Charlotte Steele (8)	9
Nathan Hunt (8)	9
Tia Henney (8)	10
Chloe Bailey (10)	10
Craig Swainson (9)	11
Serena Bailey (10)	11
Ben Bethell (11)	12
Leah Leverton (8)	12
Ethan Shea (10)	13
Caitlin Hughes (9)	13
Kimberley McKitton (10)	14
Jessie-Mai Laidler (7)	14
Lucy Turner (9)	15
Conor Hudson (9)	15
Emma Smith (8)	16
Serena Matthews (10)	16
Jamie Sansom (9)	17
Aaron Shea (8)	17
Kacie Clifton (7)	18
Christopher Harvey (11)	18
Jamie Brewer (11)	19
Ellie Biggs (8)	19
Owen Rawlins (8)	20
Charlie Green (7)	20
Lucy Gorringe (9)	21
Charlie Giblin (9)	21
Amanda Rogers (10)	22
Eleanor Bernard (8)	22
Connor-John Oak (8)	23
Zak Summerill (7)	23
Nathan Healey (8)	23
Bobbie Smith (7)	24
Sam Carter (8)	24
Benjamin Fitzpatrick (9)	24
Sam Barter & Martin Yeatman (11)	25
Natalie Edwards (7)	25
Erica Bassford (8)	25
Lewis Levy (7)	26
Harry Snape (7)	26
Morgan Bailey (8)	26

Blurton Primary School
Leighton Williams (9)	26
Jack Madigan (9)	27

Luke Bell (9) 27
Charlotte Butler (8) 27
Jack Edwards (9) 28
Harry Tudor (8) 28
Ashley Bruce (9) 28
Lennox Allen (8) 28
Mackenzie Birks (9) 29

Charnwood Primary School
Laura Bryan (11) 29
Tanesha Louise Collinson (11) 30
Jake Eyles (10) 31
Georgia Harris (11) 32
Jack Wring (11) 32
Chloe Truman (11) 33
Holly Waterhouse (11) 33
Rebbeca Wallis (10) 34
Ewan Mark Hendy (10) 34
Callum Phillips (10) 35
Abbie Curtchley (10) 35
Chloe Bickley (11) 36
Lucy Dixon (11) 36
Georgina Holt (10) 37
John Bannister (10) 37
Hugo Marvin (11) 37

Christ Church CE Middle School
Megan Young (10) 38
Imogen Rowlinson (10) 39
Eve Brown (9) 39
Caleb Barber (10) 40
Ella Webster (9) 40
R Manuell (10) 41
Verity Kingman (9) 41
Evie Darlow (10) 42
Molly Taylor (9) 43
Harmony-Jade Fuller 43

Codsall Middle School
Amee Plimmer (11) 44
Millie Warrilow (11) 45
Ellie Froggatt (10) 45
Nicholas Landon 46
Neve Hodgkins (10) 46
Scott Jones 47

English Martyrs Catholic Primary School
Oliver Jones (8) 47
Tiffany Louise Gidman (11) 48
Tia-Louise Simpson (11) 49
Summer Grace Jackson (10) 50
Lucy Whitehurst (8) 50
Leah Roden-Piper (9) 51
Macie Bell (11) 51
Seren Louise Hogan (11) 52
Kiera Hogan (10) 52
Cameron Grimes (9) 53
Naomi Lehepuu (11) 53
Dylan Jameson (9) 54
Abigail Thompson (10) 54
Rosie Cooke (8) 54
Megan Derry (9) 55

Oakhill Primary School
Charlotte Vila-Watkin (10) 55
Iona Roberts (11) 56
Stephanie Billings (11) 56
Jack Pedley (10) 57
Josiah Chilaka (11) 57
Joshua Heath-Pedley (11) 58
Grace Browning (11) 58
Chloe Overhand (11) 59
Demi Welford (11) 59
Henry Cope (11) 60
Joshua Bowers (11) 60
Holly Dean (11) 60
Olivia Daisy Jean Peters (10) 61
Jack Hawkins (11) 61

St Christopher's Catholic Primary School, Codsall
Josh Harris (11) 61
Thomas Boyce (10) 62
Katie Safrany (10) 62
Kirstie Evans (11) 63
Joe Bolton (10) 63
Liam James Murrin (11) 64
Jessica Lilly Hammond (11) 65
Hannah Dibble (11) 66
Martha Bradbury (11) 67
Orlagh Bonser (10) 68

St Michael's CE Primary School, Lichfield
Alicia Burke (10) 68
Abigail Kershaw (10) 69
Eleri Van Block (10) 70
Nina Poley (10) 71

St Paul's CE Primary School, Stafford
Charlotte Allerton-Price (11) 71
Harrison Smith (10) 72
Ethan Crompton-Jones (11) 73
Natalie Brown (11) 73
Olivia Eve Sproston (11) 74
Caitlin Samuel-Camps (9) 74
Andrew Turner (11) 75
Joseph Glayshier (9) 75
James Evans (10) 76
Fergus Adderley (10) 76
Niamh Dale (10) 77
Emily Ferguson (11) 77
Matthew Wright (10) 78
Lochlan Woolley (10) 78
Charlotte Cox (11) 79
Emily Hanson (9) 79
Joel O'Connor (11) 80
Lewis Penny-Slinn (10) 80
Joshua Elliott (9) 80

Thursfield Primary School
Junia Jai Lawson (10) 81
Aaron Oakes (10) 82
Katie Figgins (10) 82
Niamh Minton (11) 83
Harrison Berry (10) 83
Aimee Worth (10) 84
Ronan Proud (11) 84
William Wilson (10) 85
Joe Booth (11) 85
Hannah Bourne (10) 86
Charlotte Heath (10) 86
Courtney Gidman (10) 87
Callum Pugh (11) 87
Lauren Kelly (10) 88
Elleanor Cornes (10) 88
Lucie Williams (11) 88

Matthew Walker (10) 89
James Fish (11) 89

Two Gates CP School
Brendon Youlden (11) 89
Macauley Bancroft (10) 90
Jake Robbins (10) 90
Danielle Woodhouse (10) 91
Kyle Turner (10) 91
Chelsea-Jade Beale (10) 92
Emily Broadfield (10) 92
Sam Dean (10) 93
Morgan Walker (10) 93

The Poems

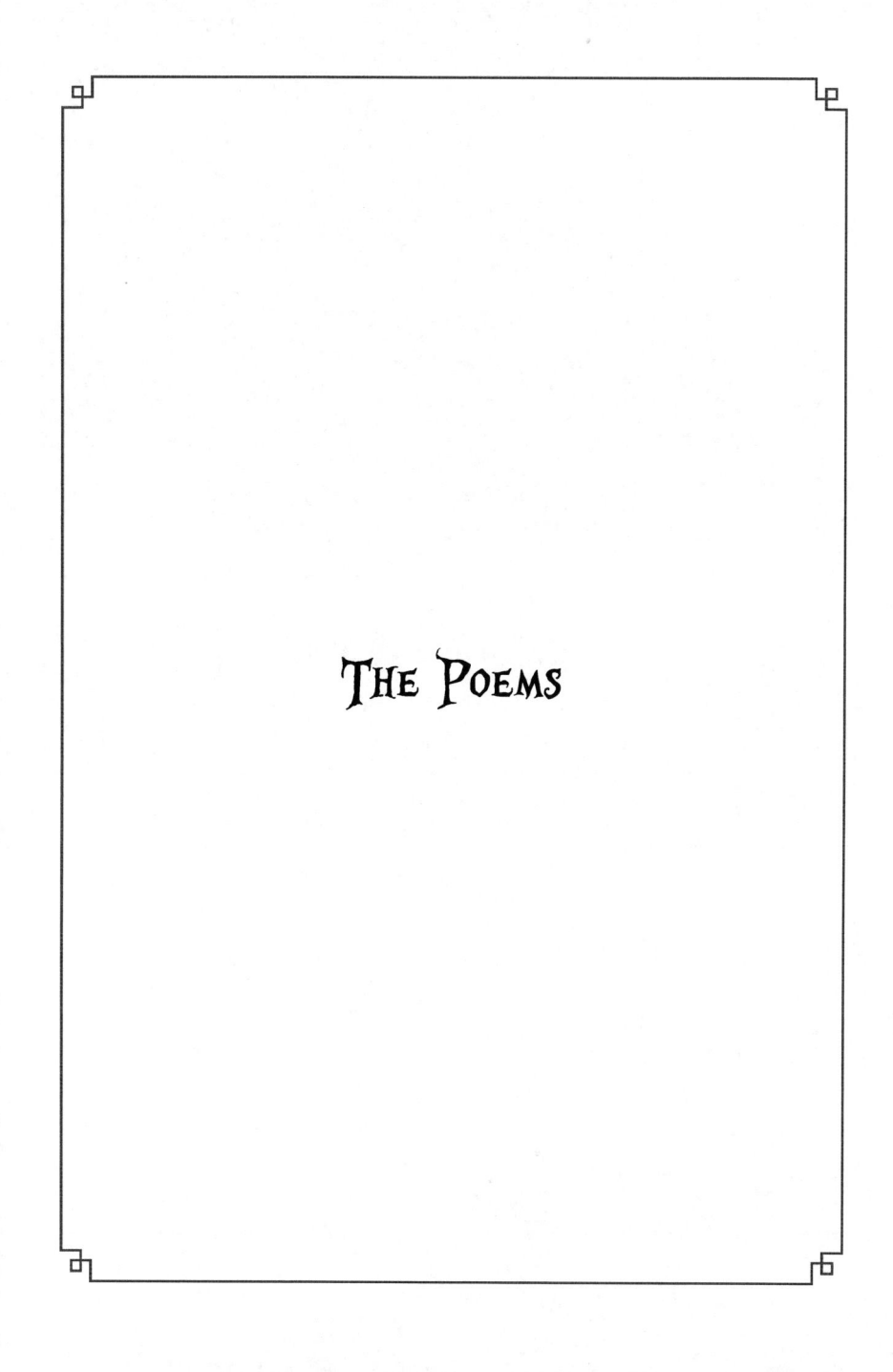

A Mighty Monument

Dusk falls,
Stone monuments stir.
Cold, hard stone turns to burning, red flesh.
Cold wings turn to bright gold,
Then him -
King of all monuments,
The Dragon.
His tail, pointed at the end,
His sharp fangs, sharp as knives,
Eyes blazing like fire.
Scales as hot as sweltering sausages,
One slash of his razor claws
Will rip to pieces
Your cold stone.
His thunderous roar raging
Through the museum,
Signalling that the coast is clear.
Coming out of their shadowy corners,
Blazing fire burning at mouths,
Lighting candles all round the museum.
They play and destroy,
They are mad.
Dawn rises,
The sun peeks through the windows,
They gallop back to their corners.
As the last monument turns back to stone
People start flooding in to see the Dragon.

Jessica Cole (9)
Birchwood Primary School

Growler

Growler is a great big puncher,
He's a gigantic beast that is a cruncher.
He lives in a stone home,
When he eats everybody he leaves no bone,
He is always on the go,
Will he eat?
Nobody knows!

Jake Calcott (7)
Birchwood Primary School

The Haunted City

The stroke of midnight they come alive
House lights turn off
They come back
The people that live there are dead
No one knew it happened
Unless it happened to you
The glass breaks everywhere
It happens at every house there is

Werewolves rise from the dead
They hide high up in the air
Staring at people walking by
They kill them without being noticed
They hide underground, in the sewers

They go to every street, they are up in the air
In the sewers underground
They hide in the corners of museums
In trees, everywhere
You don't see them though
They hide on rickety roofs, howling at the moon

People are no longer there
They won't be there forever
All have gone
They are no more
The day arrives
The werewolves have taken over.

William Ryan Gallett (8)
Birchwood Primary School

Medusa

Her eyes turn you to stone
That's why she lives all on her own
Medusa is her name
Being evil is her game
She's almost here . . .
Her eyes are cold
Her heart is bold
She has lots of stories to be told.

Pippa Randall (7)
Birchwood Primary School

Death

I watched as he did it,
Through my bedroom window.
I lay down on my bed,
Head in the pillow.

Blood spattered on the grass,
Down by the cliffside.
He ran after her,
But then she tried to hide.

I thought it was a game then,
It did look quite fun,
When I found it wasn't,
'Twas too late, *bang!* of a gun.

I ran down the stairs,
Out of the door,
But I was too late,
She was alive no more.

A big hole in her chest,
Blood cascading down and out.
I went straight back indoors,
When I was in I heard a shout.

I ran back outside again,
Thought I was there to pay,
He had a gun in his hand,
Said I was next to play . . .

Tabatha Carter (10)
Birchwood Primary School

Troll

The troll is here
It's near
It's mean
It's green
Sharp claws, poisonous hands
You'd better dash
It can kill you in a flash!

Jamie Smart (7)
Birchwood Primary School

The Haunted House Comes To Life!

Midnight. The city sleeps.
Time to escape the haunted house,
To the outskirts of the city.

Crawl into the houses
To scare people all night.
The witch and the ghost fight
About who will scare that night.

The wicked witch watches
Up in the windows,
What could be watching them?
A black figure sitting in a chair,
What could it be,
A person or a werewolf?
Oh yes, it's a werewolf!

What's he doing up there?
Scaring the children like we dare.
Now we have to fight,
We have to get our job back,
So let's get up there and start that fight.

When they're ready they go.
The werewolf's waiting,
As if he knows that they were coming.
They open the door,
That's when the fight starts.

Kelsey Anne Cunningham (8)
Birchwood Primary School

Mythical Creature Poem

Be aware if you get close to her pointy horn,
It might smash you and make your skin torn.

The Minotaur's life is in her lair,
If you dare start to stare.

In her evil and twisted eyes,
You may get hypnotised.

Billy Randall (7)
Birchwood Primary School

Ghastly Gargoyles

In the big, eerie city
Ghastly gargoyles are grazing gratefully.
In the big, eerie city
What were the giggling gargoyles doing?

Bang, crash, whoosh, pop!
There's something strange peering out.
Pop, whoosh, crash, bang!
It's got fierce, sharp teeth with
The most bumpy back and pointy ears.

As the moon goes down
And the sun comes up
Shadows appear on the buildings,
But something weird is going on.
The day goes so fast,
So the ghostly gargoyles
Come out once again!

Come out! Come out!
There's a peculiar gargoyle.
Go in, go in!
But let's not scare it.
There's a black bat
Going through the bracing fresh air.
Wibberly, wobbly skeletons just standing there.

Gargoyles rest on colossal buildings once again.

Isobel Wilson (9)
Birchwood Primary School

Mythical Creature Poem

Medusa is mean, she has snakes as hair,
Medusa and her sisters live in a lair.

Do not stare
At her wicked hair!

Her hair was made of snakes,
They were not fakes.

Shannon White (7)
Birchwood Primary School

The Baby

The day my baby sister came,
I tried to hide under my bed.
She was here to stay,
So today was the day
I moved in under my bed.
I had my precious Pillowpet,
My real cat as well,
The television set,
The Wii console.
I wasn't going down there,
Not even for a drink,
Besides, I had a can of Coke,
I had a stash of sweets,
Bubblegum and crisps,
I'm not going down there,
Nu-uh.

But soon I peered around my door
And saw a cute face,
A little tuft of hair
Covering her face.
She was actually quite cute,
I really love her now,
Might as well move back in,
Better go back down!

Chloe Bagshaw (11)
Birchwood Primary School

Chimera

You will die if you just touch him,
You will smell like a horrible pit.
You will have a fright,
As you might want a light.
You will be on your own,
So you might want to moan.
Chimera lives in a cave,
And he ate a person called Dave.
He is a deadly creature
And he wouldn't want to meet ya!

Harriett Steele (7)
Birchwood Primary School

Personification Poem

Small but strong, sharp when dropped
You can pick me up in your local shop
Both children and adults love me filled with pop!

Watch me change colour as you pour liquid into me
I turn:
White with milk
And brown with Pepsi

I have a thousand eyes
Except when the cupboard door slams
All the eye sees is darkness

I sit with my friends on a shelf in the cupboard
It's not as dusty as old Mother Hubbard's!

From the art of ancient Egypt
I am known to people across the world
I am as famous as the Queen!

The end of my life is when I smash into pieces,
A million or more
As dead as a black hole going nowhere
Never-ending, never animating, just being lifeless.

What am I?

A: A glass.

Darcie Buchan (10)
Birchwood Primary School

Medusa

Don't moan
She'll turn you to stone.
Medusa is her name,
Evil is her game.
If you dare
Have a stare,
She doesn't care,
There's snakes in her hair!
Is Medusa dead or alive?
Will she survive?

Lewis James Bell (8)
Birchwood Primary School

Haunting City

Midnight, all hushed,
Time to escape
To the smog-covered city.
Night has come,
Looking out windows,
See witches' clutching claws on walls with mossy tongues,
Empty eyes unblinking.

Creeping in people's houses,
Making noises,
Flying as high as the sky,
In the inky, black sky,
With stars glowing like the sun,
Above the city sleepers.
They look for mischief.
Bash! Bang! Wallop!
Down we go,
A girl comes to check if everything's alright,
But in the corner of her eye
She sees the ghosts.
She rushes inside, like a lion in a race.
Sun rises,
Moon fades,
Ghosts are haunting.

Laura Doak (8)
Birchwood Primary School

The Horse Who Had Paws

There was a horse that had paws
Who always broke the laws
He lived in a field
And had a shield
He went to school
And looked like a fool
He couldn't swim
And wouldn't have a hair trim
So he couldn't see
And got terrible fleas
That is all I have heard about the horse that had paws!

Stephanie Manton (10)
Birchwood Primary School

The City

Black bats swooping in the midnight air
Ugly gargoyles always think it's fair
They throw shadows down dark alleyways
Bang! Drip drop!

The roof is dripping
The door is banging
Miserable gargoyles' teeth are black and chipped
They swing in trees
With their knobbly knees.

Rrrr! Doors are creaking
In the fierce wind.
Gargoyles fly and watch the dark city
Gargoyles are as ugly as witches!

Sometimes they laugh until early morning
Owls perch on a tree, tu-whit tu-whooing
Hideous gargoyles' bloodless bodies are revolting!
They are as hard as a stone wall.
Then they fly back and perch
Just before the warm sunshine rises.

But now they are yawning
As the sunshine is coming.

Charlotte Steele (8)
Birchwood Primary School

Raging Gargoyles

Crash, bang, wallop! Gargoyles
They're as fierce as a great monster!
They swoop from trees,
They hang from buildings.

They're scary,
They're mean.

Gargoyles lurking in every corner,
Their ears are pricked up like cat's ears.

Bang! Gargoyles like bloodless bodies
Gliding through the shivering air.

Nathan Hunt (8)
Birchwood Primary School

The Haunted Devils At Night

The evening's nearly over
It's time to wake up
Let's get together
And eat some people up.

Blood is creeping out our mouths
Ready to gobble you up
Terrifying people
As long as they're asleep.

With my laser eyes
Pointing at you
Freaking you out
Nobody's seen us before.

I come out of the churchyard
Serious spiders cover me
And booming bats fly past
Going *whizz, whizz!*

So you'll never want
With ghosts and bats
Following you around
Because the house is haunted
And it still is!

Tia Henney (8)
Birchwood Primary School

Personification Poem

I cannot exist without microbes,
Give me a hot cuddle to warm me up,
Brown or white I can be,
From time to time I have spots,
Whole or sliced, I don't mind either,
I love tans as if they were my sun,
I'm in masses of different shapes,
Hard and soft I am.

What am I?

A: Bread.

Chloe Bailey (10)
Birchwood Primary School

Imaginary Gargoyles

What is that I see?
Are they gargoyles?
Ready to start mischief
As they walk down
Rickety roads of ruin.

Flip, flap
As they pass tall buildings
That are demolished and deserted.
They slither on the rocky ground
And they peer up into the sky
With no feeling.

As they smile and laugh
You see their
Black, chipped teeth.
As trees sway in the distance,
Gargoyles swing from branch to branch,
Causing mischief now and again.

As their ears prick up,
They hear the sound of morning
And quickly fly back to where they were
And turn back into their heartless selves again.

Craig Swainson (9)
Birchwood Primary School

The World's Worst Day

I had some breakfast one day and it was stale and plain.
I was about to go to the shop to get my money back,
But my mom's tyre was flat.
So I had to walk it from here to there.

When I got there the shop was shut.
It started to rain, so I had to run home.
When I got home the door was locked,
I pulled and pulled with all my might
Then the alarm went off.

When my mom finally let me in
I started crying in the sink.

Serena Bailey (10)
Birchwood Primary School

Personification

When you switch it on its heart starts beating.
At night the eyes illuminate the gloomy dark.
The brain starts thriving with things to do.
The arms heave you in when you need to go.
While the sun shines the skin reflects like ice.
Once it starts to talk or sing you cannot stop it until you turn it off.
It likes to get a drink frequently
But it does not get one until you take it.
It crawls along on its hands and knees
To get to its destination.
Its coat is so delicate
If you lay a hand on it with something sharp it will leave a scratch.
It can come in all different colours.
It can arrive in all different shapes and sizes.
It can move at so many different speeds.
Its hands and knees wear out rapidly
So it needs them to be replaced every once in a while.
It can go for miles and miles
Until it gets to its destination.

Guess what it is?

A: A car.

Ben Bethell (11)
Birchwood Primary School

Medusa

Medusa is her name
And being evil is her game
Medusa has slippy snake hair
And she has a stone lair
Her sisters were sad when Perseus cut off her head
And she fell back, for she was dead
Poor Medusa, she lived all on her own
But don't feel sorry for her, she could turn you to stone
That's why she liked to moan and groan
Sorry it's time we go
Because it's not safe here

Wow! Look at what Medusa did to that poor dear!

Leah Leverton (8)
Birchwood Primary School

One Mad Class

'Good morning everyone, let's take the . . .
Danny, no looking up Vanessa's skirt!
No Sally, you can't go to the toilet.
Kevin, I am sure that Jane can manage without you sitting on her.
Class, we are now taking the register.
Good, everyone is here.
Justin, where's your PE kit?
Vanessa no laying on the table.
Sally! Get your head out of the loo.
Ken, stop whistling.
Jack, it's not playtime yet,
Five minutes to go.
Stephen, what are you doing?
No kissing.'

Playtime
'Mrs Butcher is here with the toast and . . .
Sally, leave Jane alone,
Kenny you can't go to the toilet.

Just stop!'

Ethan Shea (10)
Birchwood Primary School

Gargoyles

As the clouds float over the city
The gargoyles peer into the midnight sky.

Gargoyles have rather rotten teeth,
Bloodless bodies roaming the dark streets,
Just watch the gargoyles silently creep,
Black bats swoop through the eerie night sky.

The gargoyles run up the rickety road,
As the statues flee,
The gargoyles tease in silent mode.

Running around, like gargoyles do,
Splish, splash, splosh!
Sound the ghastly gargoyles,
Taking the cherubs' place.

Caitlin Hughes (9)
Birchwood Primary School

Funny Animals

Cats, cats they love rats
Especially with pink, fluffy hats.
They never miss, but sometimes hiss,
Maybe they should kiss . . .

Dogs, dogs they hate frogs
When they sit on spotty logs.
They are very hairy and can dance like a fairy,
But sometimes are very scary . . .

Cows, cows they have big bells
And they like to walk on shiny shells.
When they make me milk and cheese
They normally sneeze. Oh please!

Lions, lions they love meat
They catch their dinner with their feet.
They run, jump and climb,
Hurry up, we're out of time . . .

That's all the funny animals written by me,
Join me next time, maybe? We'll see!

Kimberley McKitton (10)
Birchwood Primary School

The Chimera

Chimera is my name,
I am ready to play a game.
I have a serpent's tail,
My roar sounds like hail.
I like to sneak around,
I never make a sound,
I am as scary as can be,
I will have you for my tea.
I am very mad,
I can get very mad.
I am as quiet as can be,
I am always free.
I am half lion, half snake,
I am always awake!

Jessie-Mai Laidler (7)
Birchwood Primary School

Mischievous Gargoyles

The darkness falls and the stars come out
On the corner of a building there's a shout.

'Hey guys!' Out of character now
'We can play in the city of darkness.'
Creeping like mice
The gargoyles walk across the rickety roads of ruin.

'Cherubs, shift yourselves!'
Very sadly
The cherubs, their heads facing the floor
Get out of their places, feeling down,
The gargoyles get in with an upside down frown.

Splish, splash, splosh!
The gargoyles jump in,
Splashes of water shoot out
And splat on the floor.
The menacing gargoyles strike once more.

Lucy Turner (9)
Birchwood Primary School

The Wrath Of The Vampire

Midnight strikes again
The deadly vampires awake
Dunn-dunn-durr
He can turn into a vicious bat
To fly in the haunted house
Like security guards guarding jewellery
The vampires assassinate
The gargoyles arrive
Then, in a blink of an eye
The vampires assassinate the first gargoyle
The next assassinated -
Another gargoyle is dead
Drip-drop, dark red blood
For the vampires to drink
Mwahahahahahahaha
So back into the coffin goes the vampire
To sleep till nightfall.

Conor Hudson (9)
Birchwood Primary School

Creepy, Eerie Gargoyles

Gargoyles, gargoyles, creepy, eerie gargoyles.
Crash! Bang! Snap!

I see gargoyles,
Chipped black and yellow teeth,
Flippity flap,
There goes a bat beneath.

Creeping up tall buildings,
Never stopping for a feast,
When the day has gone
And night has begun.
We all go to play,
Us ugly beasts!

I see gargoyles, creepy, eerie gargoyles,
Running across the road,
They cause loads of mischief,
In a big load.

Emma Smith (8)
Birchwood Primary School

Personification Poem

I may stand out from other objects.
This bizarre object has millions of eyes watching you all night.
It used to live in a store, but now I'm in a drawer.
I can have a tremendously large territorial army that you may peel.
You can see me all night when you open the door,
But sometimes I can roll around in this strange drawer.
I can come in a packet of three.
You can peel me if you desire.
I have to grow on a cane all day and all night.
When I'm prepared, I'm prepared to eat.
I am hard outside and soft inside.
You can hold me but I'd rather be eaten today.
I'm hard, I'm soft, I'm rough, I'm hairy and I'm tough.

What am I?

A: Kiwi fruit.

Serena Matthews (10)
Birchwood Primary School

A Dark City With Gargoyles

Ghastly gargoyles, giggling gargoyles,
Swooping and peering over buildings.

Ghastly gargoyles, giggling gargoyles,
Breaking into buildings and making sounds like . . .
Crash, bang and *wallop!*

Ghastly gargoyles, giggling gargoyles,
Their shadows in corners.

Ghastly gargoyles, giggling gargoyles,
They love to swing on trees
And to cause chaos on tall buildings!

Ghastly gargoyles, giggling gargoyles,
Bashing down doors and turning on the light switch.

Ghastly gargoyles, giggling gargoyles,
Scaring people out of their skins
And knocking over dustbins!

Jamie Sansom (9)
Birchwood Primary School

Gazing Gargoyles

When gargoyles awake
They peer down into the city
Bang, crash, wallop!
As they scare and tease each other.

Concrete eyes peering up into the midnight sky
When the eerie beasts open their mouth
You can see the reflection
Of their chipped, old teeth.

In every corner
Their ears prick up
To hear the chaos of the city.

As morning comes
The gargoyles, on top of buildings
Freeze as hard as rock.

Aaron Shea (8)
Birchwood Primary School

The Minotaur

He is half bull, half man,
He'll catch you and eat you if he can.
Don't you dare
Go into his lair.
You're still alive,
How did you survive?
Did you fight?
Are you a knight?
Were you all alone?
He could have bitten you to the bone!
You'd better watch out,
Here comes his shout,
'I'm hungry!'
If he craves us,
I disagree!

Kacie Clifton (7)
Birchwood Primary School

The Wall

The wall's strong
The wall's weak
The wall's shiny
The wall's rusty
The wall's pretty
The wall's ugly
The wall's tall
The wall's small
The wall's wide
The wall's narrow
The wall's hard
The wall's soft
The wall's straight
The wall's bendy
And that's all about the wall.

Christopher Harvey (11)
Birchwood Primary School

The Human That Is Not Human

His skin is black and as smooth as a baby's cheek.
He likes to be cool so he breathes from the side of his head
To keep him nice and comfortable.
His arms are as skinny as twigs
But are unbelievably bendy
And his hands have only two fingers.
He has four tattoos on each hand, because he likes to be stylish.
He is fabulous at playing games
And having a brilliant time with you.
He has only one eye but he can still see very well.
He turns blue when he wants to play a game with you
And red when he is asleep but when he wakes up he winks at you.

Guess what it is?

A: PlayStation 3

Jamie Brewer (11)
Birchwood Primary School

Haunted Or What?

At the stroke of midnight
The ghosts will rise
To scare the children in the night!
They crawl and creep
To find new flesh and meat!

The night is filled with doom and gloom,
The mummy breaks out of the ancient tomb.

Spooky spirits fly so high,
Up above, in the midnight sky.
Juicy children wander by,
Eyes following all the time.
Sun will rise and the ghost will go back to hide,
They wait till night to scare and fright again.
Beware of the night!

Ellie Biggs (8)
Birchwood Primary School

The Haunted House

There is a haunted house on Creaky Lane,
The wood rattles as the wind blows.
The door goes bang when no one is there,
The blood dribbles out of the wolf's mouth.

The wind howls like a wolf,
The nails come loose on the wooden house,
I can hear the glass shatter into a million pieces,
Wolves are all over the place,
My heart misses a beat every minute.

If I were you I would stay away from the horrible doors,
The horrible wolves,
Horrible glass,
The horrible wind
And horrible lives.

Owen Rawlins (8)
Birchwood Primary School

Medusa

Snakes maybe used to a creepy lair,
But not used to Medusa's hair.
Medusa's eyes turn you to stone,
That's why she lives all on her own.
Slimey, slippy and gooey spit,
How on Earth does she manage it?
Her heart is bold,
Her eyes are cold,
When she walks she glides along,
The snakes will get hypnotised as she sings her songs.
Medusa is a powerful queen
And she is extremely mean.
Medusa is about to stare,
So you'd better not look over there.

Charlie Green (7)
Birchwood Primary School

Creepy Creatures

As creepy creatures creep quietly,
Ghastly ghosts glide like bats in dark corners,
Gargoyles causing havoc in the city,
Concrete eyes peering up into the midnight sky.

Gargoyles teasing each other tiredly,
Pigeons leaving their mess behind,
Gargoyles swinging on branches
And making each other angry.

As ghosts appear from nowhere,
They prance and dance around the world,
Singing a song.
Creepy creatures floating around,
The night brings a frightful chill once again.

Lucy Gorringe (9)
Birchwood Primary School

The Creepy House

It was a dark, wet night,
The witches scream their heads off,
They scare people, the door's going bang!
When no one is there
The tap goes *drip, drop* with blood dripping,
Then . . . the bells rings . . .

The skeleton shakes, his bones clatter,
The dog barks, he pretends that no one is there.
I hear windows crashing on the floor,
I hear children chatting inside,
I hear witches going 'Ha, ha.'
I hear gates crashing together,
I hear people slamming their car doors.

Charlie Giblin (9)
Birchwood Primary School

My Mum And Dad

M y mum is wonderful
Y ou would always love me

M y mum feeds me lots of good stuff
U seless, if I didn't have her I would be lost
M um, you are my life

A nd Dad
N o one would have a dad with love like you
D o you know how special he is to me?

D on't like it when I get told off
A nd Dad I could be happier
D ad, you are my life.

Amanda Rogers (10)
Birchwood Primary School

Mythical Creature Poem

Medusa lives in her lair,
With her evil, snake hair.

If you look at her snake
You will start to shake.

Perseus cut off her head
And she fell down, dead.

Medusa was an evil queen,
Beautiful, but very mean.

She could turn people into stone
And she was well known.

Eleanor Bernard (8)
Birchwood Primary School

The Dead City

At the stroke of midnight
In a smog-covered city
Time for the knights
Stone bodies to turn to skin and flesh
And see pharaohs wrapped in bandages
And put in tombs.

They gather round a water fountain
The knights meet friends called gargoyles
They fright in the night
And they conquer the world.

Connor-John Oak (8)
Birchwood Primary School

Medusa

Medusa's eyes turn you to stone,
When she gets angry she will moan.
Medusa has snake hair,
If you touch it you will feel despair.
Perseus cut off her head
And gave it to the dead.
She lives all alone
In a country called Rome.
She is a wicked queen
And she is always mean!

Zak Summerill (7)
Birchwood Primary School

Mythical Creature Poem

Medusa has snake hair
Don't dare to stare

If you go to her lair
Be careful not to stare

If you stare at her you turn to stone
And if you do, don't moan.

Nathan Healey (8)
Birchwood Primary School

Medusa

Medusa is like a witch,
She has horrible, hissing hair; which might itch.
She will moan,
So don't groan.
Don't go too near,
She's almost here.
Beware! She will turn you into stone,
That's why she lives on her own.
Medusa is her name,
Being evil is her game.

Bobbie Smith (7)
Birchwood Primary School

Abomanatia

A wolf's head will turn you to stone,
With super-hot lasers that will make you moan.
The Abomanatia lives on his own
Because of his terrible groan.
He always has a feast
Just because he is a beast.
He lives in a dirty heap
A heap of meat is all he eats.
The meat is as hard as stone
He will even eat your bones!

Sam Carter (8)
Birchwood Primary School

The Tiger

The tiger is the king of the beasts
The tiger that runs faster than any human
The tiger, the greatest animal on Earth
The tiger, the colours of black and orange
The tiger has the loudest roar ever!

No wonder it's called the tiger.

Benjamin Fitzpatrick (9)
Birchwood Primary School

Personification Poem

One massive eye I have lurking in the air.
Six legs scatting across the ice, leaving a sharp trail behind.
Four arms sawing into cloud
And two arms hanging outside my body with pointy fingers.
As my ribcage cracks open objects emerge from my stomach.
Rope drops down, things spin to the ground.
It has a tail with a tip that spins 100mph.

What am I?

A: An army helicopter.

Sam Barter & Martin Yeatman (11)
Birchwood Primary School

Mythical Creature Poem

How did Medusa do her hair?
Have you ever been in her lair?

She will turn you into stone,
But do not moan.

Her hair was full of snakes,
They were not fakes.

Someone cut off Medusa's head,
She dropped down, dead.

Natalie Edwards (7)
Birchwood Primary School

Mythical Creature Poem

Even if his tummy feels full,
He can still roar like an angry bull.

The Minotaur's favourite food is meat,
He also has gigantic feet.

The Minotaur has a razor-sharp horn,
Metal can be easily torn.

The Minotaur can breathe fire,
Also he can make you tire.

Erica Bassford (8)
Birchwood Primary School

Dethicas

Dethicas, why are you so jealous?
Scorpion tail could scratch you,
The piranha heads will make you go to bed,
Your bat ears can hear a cat,
The skunk tail is toxic,
It really makes you yell.

Lewis Levy (7)
Birchwood Primary School

Medusa

Perseus cut off her head
And then she fell, stone dead.
Horrible, hissing hair
That you could never bear!
Nobody would ever dare
To touch her horrible, hissing hair.

Harry Snape (7)
Birchwood Primary School

Medusa

Medusa is my name
How I like to play the game!
My hair rattles like a snake
Can you see it shake?
I live on my own, in a creepy cave
It is the place I call home.

Morgan Bailey (8)
Birchwood Primary School

Anger

Anger is like a dragon that has got a temper
Anger is like a volcano ready to erupt
It is like a tormented bull
Getting ready to start charging at you.

Leighton Williams (9)
Blurton Primary School

Love

Love is like a moonlit lake
Love is like an angel shooting you in the back
Love is like you're already in Heaven
Love is like a romantic night for a loving pair
Love is like a radiant, tropical island
Love is like a wife's valentine
Love is like a gentle, blue ocean.

Jack Madigan (9)
Blurton Primary School

Heartbroken

Like the colour in your heart has faded away
Like your heart can't be repaired
Like your body has been shut down
Like a tsunami washing your happiness away
Like your heart has been blown into a million pieces
Like a black hole sucking all your love away
Like your heart is burning up.

Luke Bell (9)
Blurton Primary School

Love

Love is like a river flowing to joy,
Love is like a teddy bear cuddling you,
Love is like a romantic dinner on a cruise,
Love is like a person feeling very energetic,
Love is like flying in the clouds,
Love is like your heart is beating one hundred times,
Love is like you're dreaming of a nice day.

Charlotte Butler (8)
Blurton Primary School

Anger

Anger is like a bull charging into your back
Like your heart is ready to explode
Like horns stabbing into your head
Like a lion hunting for its prey
Like a bull in a red box
Like a volcano ready to erupt
Like lightning striking your happiness away.

Jack Edwards (9)
Blurton Primary School

Anger

As angry as a dragon pouncing on its prey
Like a devil's eyes staring at its prey
Like a bull in a red box
Like a lion hunting for its prey
Like lightning striking you
As angry as a volcano erupting.

Harry Tudor (8)
Blurton Primary School

Anger

Anger is like a vulture scratching your eyes out
Like a jaguar ripping you apart
As angry as a bull in a red box
Like horns stabbing you in the head
As angry as a hawk
Like lightning striking your happiness away.

Ashley Bruce (9)
Blurton Primary School

Loneliness

Loneliness is like no one is there for you, it's heartbreaking
Loneliness is like being washed away
Loneliness is like your heart is melting
Loneliness is like being stranded on a desert island.

Lennox Allen (8)
Blurton Primary School

Anger

It's like a volcano erupting
It's like a fierce dragon
Like lightning striking your happiness away
Like a lion hunting for its prey
Like a bull charging into your back
Like horns stabbing you in the head.

Mackenzie Birks (9)
Blurton Primary School

My Imaginary World

My houses are made of candy,
Now this is very handy,
As, if you get hungry just pull down a brick,
Give it a slurp, give it a gulp then give it a lick.

I live in a beautiful castle,
With ivory draped on the wall,
So look up, you'll see
It goes up so incredibly tall.

Around my village the people all bow down to me,
However, spend most of my time watching TV,
Everyone drives around in style,
In booster cars that zoom a mile.

We don't have paths, we don't have roads,
But we have mushrooms, we have toads,
No paths, no more, we put them in the dump,
Now we drive differently, we jump!

The fuel is not diesel or petrol, *no way!*
Fairy cakes is what we use, I'll say,
Chocolate is the only thing to eat,
There's no fruit, sweets, bread or meat.

All there's left to say,
This year, this month, this day,
If you like chocolate and you are a girl,
Come and visit my imaginary world!

Laura Bryan (11)
Charnwood Primary School

What Pet

I want a pet, but what pet should I have?
There are hundreds to choose from.

Let's see . . .
There are energetic pets, like dogs,
Or pets that live in stables, like horses,
Horses have to be ridden at least six times a week,
Ummm, maybe not a horse.

Now maybe a cat, as they seem fine,
But cats are so independent
And you can't have any quality walks with them,
Not a cat, as they're not the pet I want.

What about an elephant?
You hardly have to lift a finger for them,
But . . .
They're as enormous as a house
And I'm a midget,
Better not get an elephant
As I don't want to get squashed!

Now, there is one pet that I really like,
They're energetic and really loyal,
I can have quality walks with them,
their food is a bit expensive,
but so what?
There are loads of different breeds,
But my favourite is
A Border Collie cross Staffie,
In second place is
A German Shepherd cross Staffie,
Do you know what my dream pet is?

It's a dog!

Tanesha Louise Collinson (11)
Charnwood Primary School

Music

Red guitars, white guitars,
Guitars are great.
You need a lot of fate
To play the bass,
If you're in the wrong
Music puts you in your place.
Blue guitars, green guitars,
Guitars need stars.

People like Slash,
Boy, he's a bash.
Ozzy is mad,
Then there's MJ, who's bad.

Next there's drums,
But they're all fun.
People like Tre-Cool,
He's not done,
He's in Green Day
Along with Billie
And Mr. Mike Dirnt,
They all smoke,
I'm surprised they're not burnt.

Some people play keyboard,
Quite a lot,
Iron Maiden rode Concorde
And got them there in a dot.
There's rock,
Rap,
R 'n' B
Heavy metal, but that's just some,
And that's a rap, my son.

Jake Eyles (10)
Charnwood Primary School

Animals

Animals are cute, spiky or furry,
Some can be playful,
Some can be wild,
Some can be calm,
Some live on a farm.

Animals are soft, bouncy or hyper,
Some can be slow,
Some can be fast,
Some can be small,
Some can be tall.

Animals are calm, nervous or excited,
Some can be spiky,
Some can be bouncy,
Some do high jumps,
Some have two humps.

Animals are special, fun or loyal,
Some are furry,
Some are loyal,
Some love to play,
We see them nearly every day.

Georgia Harris (11)
Charnwood Primary School

Guinea Pigs

G iant teeth gnawing on lettuce
U ndisputed guinea pigs bite each other
I ce-coloured guinea pigs frolic about
N inja-like guinea pigs like to evade teeth
E cstatic guinea pigs play in the hay
A wesome tasting lettuce satisfies pigs

P ower-packed pigs tug on the cage bars
I diotic owners get mauled by them
G uinea pigs are colossally lazy
S ome are vicious.

Jack Wring (11)
Charnwood Primary School

My Friends

My friends stick with me,
My friends make me laugh.
True friends stay with you just like Abbie,
She does too, her laugh is so sweet.

My friend Holly is cool,
But she can act like a big fool,
That's why she is my friend.

Lucy is a good friend,
Just like Libby and Sue are too,
Always there to support you.

Sweet as a cherry
Is one of my friends,
Brittney, she has red glasses.

I have lots of friends,
Georgia, Tanesha, Leah, Laura, Victoria,
Isabell, Rebecca and Chloe B too.

That is all of my friends
Who help me through thick and thin,
I am so lucky!

Chloe Truman (11)
Charnwood Primary School

My Friends

My friend is called Eve,
Funny, pretty, makes me smile,
Always helping me.

My friends are so cool,
My friends love me like Chloe T,
True friends stay for life.

My best friend, Catherine,
Crazy but still my best friend,
The best friend ever.

Holly Waterhouse (11)
Charnwood Primary School

I Love Food

Food, food, love the smell
Keeps the thought that chips taste well
Chicken for my Sunday dinner
Making it a one-all winner!
Crisps and chocolate for a snack
So tasty that I have to go back
A seaside hot-dog is all I need
When I can walk the dog as he pulls on the lead
Now that's not fair!
In the evening I like a Chinese
Now I can have some prawn crackers that please
At the weekend for my tea, I like spaghetti
And that's alright
So down to McDonald's to get a hamburger, big bite
Mmm . . . yum
At school, for my dinner, I have a lovely packed lunch
Although it is not as delicious as a tasty, big brunch
Because on my birthday I love a cake
I have to have my favourite flake
Now because all that cake is gone
There is no more food left down for my mum.

Rebbeca Wallis (10)
Charnwood Primary School

Frustrating, Fabulous Football

Football is a great sport
Often people go and support
The players get ready
Whilst the opponents dive steady
The referee starts the game
The player dives, insane!
After the game the supporters go home
The team that wins is so delighted
It has to be Man United!

Ewan Mark Hendy (10)
Charnwood Primary School

Famous People

F amous people, not all do boast
A s for N-Dubz they just sing loads
M obo Awards, for singers around the world
O 2 Arena, where the Brits last time were held
U sing your time for X Factor
S ee if you become rich, you won't need a tractor

P estering the world until you get noticed
E ntertaining TV actors, embarrassed once kissed
O ver the top with screen hogging
P urposely annoying watchers when slobbing
L eaving the studios just past midnight
E ntering the sleeping world, do not have a fright.

Red carpet walking tomorrow,
Lots of cameras, lots of microphones
And questions ready to be answered,
Revealed at the advert screen only once
They always get a response.

Callum Phillips (10)
Charnwood Primary School

Animals

A nimals
N iceness to animals that need our love
I love animals
M is for mammals
A nts
L ions that roar all the time
S lithering snakes

A nteaters are huge, round, chubby and eat loads of ants
R abbits that love carrots
E normous elephants

C ruel to animals
U nicorns can grant you a wish
T all and small
E lephants are huge and let you ride on their back.

Abbie Curtchley (10)
Charnwood Primary School

Tinkerbell Is Here

T inkerbell is here
I n Pixie Hollow
N eeding to impress
K eeping all the fairy dust
E veryone needs her help
R iding the waves to the mainland
B ringing spring, summer, autumn
E ven though you can't see them
L ittle fairies are here
L iving right amongst us

I f a fairy is spotted
S omeone dies in Neverland

H ere on the mainland
E veryone is poison
R uining their work, making
E veryone in Neverland upset.

Chloe Bickley (11)
Charnwood Primary School

Oh I Wish I'd Looked After My Teeth

Oh I wish I'd looked after my teeth,
All the plaque and the dirt beneath,
Waiting to sit in the dentist's chair,
I always feel the greatest despair.

The dentist tries to hide the needle
That will make my face so numb,
The dentist thinks he's fooled me,
Does he think I'm that dumb?

Faster the time is getting,
Curious and upsetting,
Just as I think things can't get worse,
I hear my name called by the nurse.
Oh, I wish I'd looked after my teeth.

Lucy Dixon (11)
Charnwood Primary School

Animals

A is for animals living all around us, playing in the living room, tumbling all around.
N ext to that different types of animals are just like that.
I love to have a guinea pig, but instead, it will have to be a skinny pig.
M eeting all the animals would be a wonder, instead of that I have a lucky number.
A ll of you might think I am bonkers, but pigs are just like gigs.
L isten up, leopards are so spotty you'll have to go potty.
S o over all spots will get you dots.

Georgina Holt (10)
Charnwood Primary School

Maradona

M aradona did 'the hand of God'
A t the 1978 World Cup
R unning around like a headless chicken
A fter the cheated game England were out
D own under England got told off with shouts
O n the plane back to England
N o one was happy because of him,
A n ugly man who should have changed sport!

John Bannister (10)
Charnwood Primary School

Games

Games are fun,
There's something for everyone.
Also you can go on two player and online.
My games I go on are 'Halo Reach' and 'Halo 3'.
Exciting and addictive,
Something to play every day.

Hugo Marvin (11)
Charnwood Primary School

Seasons

I woke up one bright, sunny morning,
Spring had begun and winter had ended.
It was nice to wake up with no hats and scarf,
It was nice to wake up with a bright, blue sky.
There was no frost on the windows,
Instead they were clear and no frost in sight.
I got dressed in my T-shirt and shorts
And ran to the door,
I couldn't wait to smell the spring fresh air
And see fields of grass.
I was so excited that I cracked a smile on my face,
I opened the door and . . .

The earth had shaken off its winter coat,
There was green grass that covered the fields.
Wow! What a beautiful sight,
I jumped outside and hugged the air,
I ran on the fields with no snow to see.
This is the best summer there has ever been!

Two months had gone very quickly, it was autumn,
But still the sun in sight,
I could still sense spring coming back next year.
I was so excited for the next day.
But . . .
I woke up again, so excited, I ran downstairs like a gust of wind,
I opened the door and . . .
It was white everywhere, white covered the field,
White covered the house, I fell to the ground.
But still snow didn't stop me,
I made a snowman and played snowball fights.
I realised that I love the snow and I love the sun,
I love the leaves that crumple under your feet.

Megan Young (10)
Christ Church CE Middle School

The Box

The box . . .
A marvellous mystery to be found.
When I opened the box
All I could hear was a sound
Nothing was there
But I had to make sure.
I stuck my head in
And saw a sharp dragon's claw.
Someone pushed me in
I could hardly breathe
Then they closed the lid
With a massive heave.
My body was tingling
Like a huge balloon
I couldn't pop it
Someone, please stop it, *stop it!*
I couldn't get out, but
I tried and I tried
I tried to stay calm and
I cried and I cried.
The sound suddenly stopped
And I woke from my bed.
I sat up,
I rubbed my eyes
I realised
It was all in my head!

Imogen Rowlinson (10)
Christ Church CE Middle School

Dirty Dogs

Dirty dogs dig
Round the pig,
Hide like a cheeky monkey,
Which are sometimes chunky.
Disgusting dogs dream,
Like a puff of steam,
Rolling in the mud,
On a clump of chud.

Eve Brown (9)
Christ Church CE Middle School

Dragon

Dragon
Was harder
Than a concrete block.
Crawled around the misty land,
Scales like triangle stones,
Hid in a dark cave,
Flames came out of his mouth,
Flames scorched his back,
Powerful wings tried to fly,
But he is too shy.

Dragon
Was amazing at flying
He glides like a bird,
He slices through the sky like a knife through butter
And never ever stutters.
He is as long as a limousine,
Also as tall as Big Ben,
In a box of doom,
As strong as a rock
And as hot as a fire.

Dragon whines - *roar, roar, roar!*

Caleb Barber (10)
Christ Church CE Middle School

My Rhyme

I am very colourful, sometimes have a bow,
I am worn on your feet and sometimes glow.
Here, I will give you a clue . . .
I have laces, straps and other things too
And I come in twos.
I can get very smelly
(And so can you)
Everyone has a pair,
You must too.

Ella Webster (9)
Christ Church CE Middle School

Half And Half Land

Half and half land
A land not found
Half and half animals
Never to be found
A half rhinoceros
Half hippopotamus
Lazing on the muddy bank
Half eagle, half weasel
Digging a hole in the mountainside
Half cat, half rat
Sniffing and sneaking around
Half dog, half hog
Searching in the dark
Half mouse, half louse
As small as the end of your fingertips
Half fox, half ox
Standing with its rubber nose in the air
Half and half animals nobody can see
But of course, only for you and me!

R Manuell (10)
Christ Church CE Middle School

Pets

Scurrying around the bedded hutch,
My guinea pigs love it very much.

Nibbling at his plentiful food,
My hamster's in a yummy mood.

Bounding around the fertile field,
My rabbit is a fluff-ball shield.

Prowling around Nature's mud,
My cat rolls over with a thud.

Chasing around his playful mate,
My dog never gets at all irate.

When all my pets have gone to bed,
They wish a goodnight and rest their heads.

Verity Kingman (9)
Christ Church CE Middle School

Mac

Mac,
You came into our lives as a surprise,
We didn't know you were coming,
But when you did
We realised you were going to be stunning.

Mac,
You walk with a bounce,
You play ball,
You like to pounce.

Mac,
I love it now you're here,
Will always keep you near,
You jump so high,
Even manage to reach the table,
But most of all, Mac,
You love your mum,
Maybelle.

Evie Darlow (10)
Christ Church CE Middle School

The Weregirl

She slowly slinks through the forest,
No sound but her jingling things
Her eyes are small and beady
As she spies a flutter of wings.

Pads to the top of the cliff face,
Then calls her werewolf call,
Her call is directed
To the big, full moon ball.

Soon the werewolves are coming
Are sitting all around,
They want to hear the stories
This strange wolf-girl has found.

'We must not let them see me,'
She whispers to the wolves,
'You know that if they find me,
There will be no more balls!'

Molly Taylor (9)
Christ Church CE Middle School

Dragon

Dragon
Was dancing in mid-air
Swishing, swirling and swashing
Scales shone, glowing brightly
Fire spread amongst the forest
Wide-eyed
Wings gliding in the moonlight.

Dragon
Was feared
Causing trouble
Through the dazzling light
Muscling his way through towns
Villages were quiet and still
And dragon flew away
Thinking about the world ahead.

Dragon flew - *swish, swash, swirl.*

Harmony-Jade Fuller
Christ Church CE Middle School

Beans

Have you ever thought about beans?
Have you looked into it?
Do you know what it means?

First of all let's start with jelly,
It's not really a bean,
But it's yummy in my belly.

Then of course there's the bean called string,
It's really the best bean
And it should be crowned king.

Now there's the wonderful coral
To find the perfect bean,
Now that's the moral.

Now onto the jumping bean,
It jumps so fast,
It's rarely been seen.

Onto the strange and exciting red,
All those myths and legends
And mysteries that are said.

How could we forget the famous bean named black,
There's lots more beans to discover,
I quite like the bean Jack.

There's a quite nice bean called broad,
I do love all these beans,
There's even one called sword!

Long and stringy a green bean's quite nice,
I have them all the time,
They're quite nice with rice.

All this information may be really useless,
You may never use it,
But it is better than being clueless.

Amee Plimmer (11)
Codsall Middle School

Months And Seasons

January, February to the middle of March
Standing in the cold, oh the weather is so harsh
Let's make snowmen, sledge down a hill
Wintertime, wintertime, time to chill.

April, May to the middle of June
Sitting in the garden mid-afternoon
Enjoying the pretty flowers
Springtime, springtime for showers.

July, August, middle of September
Weather so hot that I'll always remember
Lying on a Lilo, long summer days
Summertime, summertime, catching the rays.

October, November, middle of December
Christmas time which you should remember
Let's watch the leaves fall, make sure you're awake
Autumn time, autumn time, time for a rake.

Let's cheer for the seasons all through the year
When one leaves another one appears
You've got to love the seasons, each is a ball
Wintertime, springtime, summertime, fall!

Millie Warrilow (11)
Codsall Middle School

School Days

On Mondays I'm still very tired,
But at least I'm a pupil so I can't get fired.

On Tuesdays we have ICT,
But all of the numbers on the screen laugh out loud at me.

Wednesday is a normal school day,
Except for art, where we have to put on a play.

On Thursdays I'm supposed to be athletic,
But I'm so tired that I just crawl along looking pathetic.

On Friday the final bell is like music to our ears,
We are all relieved and shout out lots of cheers!

Ellie Froggatt (10)
Codsall Middle School

Days Of The Week

Monday I can't play on my Wii,
But I've completed every game you see,

Tuesday is probably my favourite day,
History, art, rubbish? No way!

Wednesday I go swimming and get water up my nose,
I prefer being sprayed with the water hose.

Thursday I go to scouts and stay up late
That's great, but then going to bed I hate!

Friday is the day of bliss,
The weekend I would never miss.

Saturday is the first day of TV time,
Now I'm running out of things to rhyme.

Sunday is homework day,
But I want to play!

Nicholas Landon
Codsall Middle School

Untitled

On Monday mornings my first lesson's science,
We're learning about electrical suppliance.

On Tuesday my second lesson's French,
I'd rather stare at a park bench.

On Wednesday my third lesson's PE,
Everyone was throwing rugby balls at me.

On Friday my fifth lesson's English,
We're still personifying a golden fish.

On Saturday I finally can chill out,
Until my mom starts to shout!

On Sunday my feet are strung across the bed,
It's school tomorrow, a tear I shed.

Neve Hodgkins (10)
Codsall Middle School

Untitled

The stretch on Monday morning always keeps me yawning.
Tuesday keeps me busy, but hard exercise isn't easy.
Wednesday I'm a bit stressed, a long day without much rest.
Thursday I like the home run, because next it's Friday's fun.
Friday has bad lessons, but there's less aggression.
Saturday we live for, but there's homework, a killer bore.
Homework plus Sunday doesn't make a fun day.
There's my normal week, a new life I don't seek.

Scott Jones
Codsall Middle School

The Boxing Man

Boxing, boxing
The boxing man
Boxing, boxing
The fighting man

Boxing, boxing
The skipping man
Boxing, boxing
The dancing man

Boxing, boxing
I love the sport
Boxing, boxing
People like it

It's a good sport
Boxing, boxing
It is good
Boxing, boxing
Is the one

Boxing, boxing
It's the one for me.

Oliver Jones (8)
English Martyrs Catholic Primary School

Football

Football, football,
Gotta put your socks on,
Put your studs and kit on
Then you're done.

Come on lads,
Hurry up and dribble,
Gotta volley it
Into the goal.

Scoring, scoring,
Stoke City are the best,
Port Vale are the worst
And Man U are alright.

Munching, munching,
It's half-time now,
2-0 to Stoke
We can win now.

Second half has
Already started,
3-0 to Stoke
Yeah, yeah, yeah!

Britannia Stadium,
Is roaring with cheers,
'Cause everybody knows that
Stoke are gonna win now.

The match has finished,
We have won,
I knew we would,
Now I'm off to the pub!

Tiffany Louise Gidman (11)
English Martyrs Catholic Primary School

My Family

Jack, Darren, Mum and me,
This is my family.
We all live in a big house,
That doesn't have a single mouse.

First, let's introduce Mum,
She's a nurse,
It fills her purse,
But if I'm ill, she says it could be worse.

Then there's Darren,
He's a paramedic and pathetic.
Darren is almost bald
And never usually answers when he's called.

Finally, there's Jack,
He likes to play on his PS3
And only leaves it when he needs a wee,
Jack always talks to his mates at any rate.

Now for my pets,
There's Charlie and Henri,
They're both loopy when they wanna
But as for my hamster he was a gonna.

Rabbits, dogs, parrots and hamsters I've had,
People must think my family's mad.
I can tell you this, we are not,
It's just we've had an awful lot.

Oh, but now I've forgotten me,
Just so you know, I'm still in school,
With my friends that are really cool,
I hang with them on Friday in the pool.

Tia-Louise Simpson (11)
English Martyrs Catholic Primary School

Funny Bunny

Funny Bunny likes to laugh,
He likes to laugh a lot in class.
Oh no, naughty Funny Bunny.

Funny Bunny likes to talk,
He likes to talk to his fork!
Oh no, naughty, weird Funny Bunny.

Funny bunny likes to play,
He likes to play at the park.
Oh no, naughty, weird, hurt Funny Bunny.

Funny Bunny likes TVs,
He likes to watch TV and play on his PC.
Oh no, naughty, weird, square-eyed Funny Bunny.

Funny Bunny likes a lot,
He likes loads of things to beat the price,
Talking to his friends . . .
Oh no, naughty, weird, hurt, square-eyed,
Quiet Funny Bunny.

Summer Grace Jackson (10)
English Martyrs Catholic Primary School

Flowers

Flowers are fluffy and smell so nice,
Roses are red and violets are blue,
Buttercups are yellow
And daisies are white
And smell so nice.
Crunchy flowers are beautiful,
They smell just like shampoo.
Curly, crafty flowers, yellow
Or black, there are different sorts.
They all smell nice and of autumn, crispy and new.
Old flowers break apart, they smell so nice.
Water them once a day,
Yellow, orange, black, purple, white,
Colours of crispy ones.
People pick flowers so they can smell them.

Lucy Whitehurst (8)
English Martyrs Catholic Primary School

Family

My sister is Laura-Jo
She likes to come and go.

Jr is my brother
And he loves my mother.

Sharon is my mother
And she loves my baby brother.

Mike is my father
He works at Alton Towers all day
And when he gets home he shouts, hooray!

Wayne is my other father
And he loves my loving mother.

Major is my doggy
And he is very, very fluffy.

And then there is me
I am Leah
I like to shout and cheer.

Leah Roden-Piper (9)
English Martyrs Catholic Primary School

Best Friends Forever!

My best friend is a daydreamer
But while watching horror movies she's a screamer.

She's my bezzie forever
Even through nasty weather.

My best friend likes to shop
If she could, she would shop till she drops.

She is always in Primark
She stalks me like a shark.

Her favourite colour is purple,
Her favourite shape is a circle.
This girl is my best friend
And our love will never end.

Macie Bell (11)
English Martyrs Catholic Primary School

My Family

There's me, my sister, Mum and Dad
We all live together in one big house
Without one single louse.

The love we have will never, ever end
My mum's nice, with lots of advice.

My sister's name is Kiera
We never love each other
Even though my family think we do.

My mum's name is Kate, she loves my family very much
Sometimes we have a bit of fun
But sometimes it goes too far
And my mum gets a bit angry.

My dad's name is Tom
He's a smart business man
His help is very reassuring.

Seren Louise Hogan (11)
English Martyrs Catholic Primary School

The Frenemy

The best friend,
Didn't pretend,
That she was normal,
Because she knew she was abnormal.

The other friend
Knew that her best friend would never mend,
It was the end,
For her and her best friend.

When she told her,
They were older,
But they always knew
They were best friends all the way through.

Kiera Hogan (10)
English Martyrs Catholic Primary School

Football

Aiden, Mum, Dad and me
Went to watch Stoke and Chelsea
We rushed to find our seat
It's at the end of the week

They have just scored a gaol
A miracle one from Ashley Cole
The crowd went wild, they were on their feet
Clapping their hands, starting to leap

We were on the left hand wing
All the crowd have started to sing
'Come on Jones, use your head,
head the ball as we have said.'

Cameron Grimes (9)
English Martyrs Catholic Primary School

Best Friends

This girl is Barbie in disguise
She makes me feel right inside
She makes me laugh
But never makes me cry
She's the best, I wonder why?
This girl has got fashion taste
I'm glad it doesn't go to waste
This girl is my friend forever
Even through nasty weather
Even though her favourite colour is green
She is never mean.
Overall she's the best.

Naomi Lehepuu (11)
English Martyrs Catholic Primary School

Boys Are Better Than Girls

Boys rule better than girls
Boys are smarter than girls
Boys are faster than girls
Boys are stronger than girls
Boys have more skills than girls
Boys have more stamina than girls
Boys are cooler than girls
Boys are more awesome than girls
Boys rule, girls drool
Boys are better chefs than girls
Boys are better in statue games than girls.

Dylan Jameson (9)
English Martyrs Catholic Primary School

Love

Love, love, love, love
Love is like a river that never dries up.
Love works in many ways,
Love is like a tree,
Love shines through the dark,
Love runs on and on and on.
Love shines through the dark for me,
Love is the lock,
I am the key.
Love, love, love, love.

Abigail Thompson (10)
English Martyrs Catholic Primary School

School poem

I went to school
I had a good time
School is fun
We learn to rhyme
I like to hear the dinner bell chime
It is fun and joyful
Most of the time.

Rosie Cooke (8)
English Martyrs Catholic Primary School

My Dog

My dog is cute as a button
She licks your face in the night.
If I am sad Lilly keeps me company
She keeps me warm like a fur coat.
And she runs after cats and birds
But she can't catch them.
She runs around like a headless chicken
And she likes gin,
But I love her.

Megan Derry (9)
English Martyrs Catholic Primary School

Kennings

Giggle juice drinker
Happy winker
Spaghetti slurper
Barely burper
Secret keeper
Chocolate sneaker
Animal lover
Miserable cover
Rosy-red cheeks
Patient with weeks
Everyone's friend
Round the bend
Adores pink
Loves ink.

Who am I?

Charlotte Vila-Watkin (10)
Oakhill Primary School

Girls In Summer

Hot guys
Toned thighs
Lemonade
In the shade
Flip-flops
Jelly tots
Ice lolly
Girl's dolly
Flowers blooming
Sunscreen splatting
Big splash
Party bash
Now autumn's come
Goodbye sun!

Iona Roberts (11)
Oakhill Primary School

Free Verse

Undersea creatures
Absorbent as can be
Restaurant worker
He'll cook something for tea.

Yellow, squidgy dude
He's as funny as he can
When he's at work
He's always flippin' a pan.

Lives in a pineapple
Under the sea
Who is he?

SpongeBob SquarePants!

Stephanie Billings (11)
Oakhill Primary School

There's Something Out There

Blood drinker
Bone crusher
Night stalker
People craver
Day sleeper
Shadow lover
Human taker
Neck biter
Mayhem maker
Day ender
Bone grinder
Heart stopper
Building shaker.

Jack Pedley (10)
Oakhill Primary School

Robber

Diamond stealer
Gun user
Jail breaker
Police fighter
Handcuff hater
Hostage taker
Shop lifter
Crime lover
Money maker
Law breaker.

What am I?

A: A robber!

Josiah Chilaka (11)
Oakhill Primary School

The Osbournes

T he craziest family ever!
H ellraisers!
E ven heavier than metal!

O zzy Osbourne
S kull scratchers
B orn crazy
O n the metal
U nder blood walls
R olling in a limo
N o stopping them
E nd up in trouble
S haron!

Joshua Heath-Pedley (11)
Oakhill Primary School

What Am I?

Hay eater
Showjumper
Playful bucker
Cross-country runner
Carrot muncher
Stable sleeper
Field lover
Show winner
Rosette collector.

What am I?

A: a horse.

Grace Browning (11)
Oakhill Primary School

Ghosts

Gliding above the floor,
Scaring people to death,
Sometimes monks, sometimes not,
Not see-through but transparent,
Only one word . . .
Found in hallways,
In haunted castles,
Rattling chains,
Creaking floorboards,
Only one word . . .

Boo!

Chloe Overhand (11)
Oakhill Primary School

What Am I?

Grass eater
Water drinker
Slow runner
Fast muncher
Milk giver
Lazy sleeper
Sound maker
Messy eater
Field lover.

What am I?

Demi Welford (11)
Oakhill Primary School

What Am I

Desert racer
Vegetable murderer
Desert explorer
Cow hater
Desert roamer
Galaxy ruler
Whoa shouter
Carrot commander.

What am I?

Henry Cope (11)
Oakhill Primary School

Happiness

Happiness is sunny
With pinches of excitement
It's the best kind of feeling
That you'd want
It tastes like rich ice cream
With raspberry sauce
And it feels like soft, fleecy blankets
It smells like daffodils in the summer.

Joshua Bowers (11)
Oakhill Primary School

Bear Hunter

Bears, bears, we're looking for some bears.
Bears, bears, I think I've spotted one there,
Bears, bears, giving us a stare,
Bears, bears, we're not scared.
Growl
Snap
Argh
Yummy!

Holly Dean (11)
Oakhill Primary School

Animals

A nimals are so cute
N o mess in the kitchen
I love to be fussed
M y name is Sky
A nd I love my owner
L oves walks
S o cute.

Olivia Daisy Jean Peters (10)
Oakhill Primary School

Monsters

M ayhem maker
O utside prowler
N ight stalker
S hadow taker
T eeth grinder
E nding days with blood and gore
R ed or blue, it's coming for you!

Jack Hawkins (11)
Oakhill Primary School

Pokémon

Starapter
He is a flying type
As fast as a Bugatti
And as strong as a tank.

Torterra
He is a grass and ground type
As big as a Monster Truck
And as powerful as an army.

Insernape
He is a fire and fighting type
As brave as a knight fighting a dragon
And as blazing as a giant fire.

Josh Harris (11)
St Christopher's Catholic Primary School, Codsall

My Favourite Things Poem

The things I like to see:
I like to see the sea crashing against the sharp, ragged rocks.
I like to watch my watch that goes *tick-tock, tick-tock*.
I like to watch the sunset for the clouds go wild and pink
Just like a colour-changing chameleon.

The things I like to hear:
I like to hear the sound of dogs barking as the day rolls on
I like to hear the sound of people laughing out loud for it makes me happy.
I like to hear the sound of the schoolbell for lunch when I am hungry.

The things I like to smell:
I like to smell the scent of a bee's happy honey
I like to smell the smell of freshly baked bread
I like to smell the mown grass which is green.

The things I like to touch:
I like to touch a softy silky item for they are softer than a baby's skin
I like to touch a spoon that is about to eat some ice cream
I like to touch my PlayStation remote to play games
I like to turn on my PlayStation so I can play.

I like lots of things but I love my family and school!

Thomas Boyce (10)
St Christopher's Catholic Primary School, Codsall

Over-Heated Earth

The world is over-heated,
As hot as the sun, it soon shall be,
Sizzle! Pop! Crackle! Burn!
Soon the Earth shall explode.

Litter lying everywhere,
The sea is boiling.
The evaporated tears of the Earth cry
Save us now.

The sizzling sun,
A close contestant for the hottest planet of all,
Will anything survive?

Katie Safrany (10)
St Christopher's Catholic Primary School, Codsall

Horrible Holidays

Lucy Love was walking by the pool
Until she felt wet and cool
She opened her eyes
And said, 'How did I get here, guys?'

The swimming pool started shaking and waving
He said, 'I am hungry and there is something I am craving.'

The swimming pool made a water whale
The bed said, 'Flatten that down' and now it's a sail.

Lucy Love got out of the pool
She was so tired she had to crawl
The Coke machine said, 'Have you heard that song?
I'll sing it to you whilst we're playing ping-pong, listen.

Just gonna stand there and here me roar
That's alright because I am a dinosaur.

The chorus was sung by Rihanna
I'm obsessed, I've got me own banner.

Kirstie Evans (11)
St Christopher's Catholic Primary School, Codsall

The Lion

The first sorrow of the lion,
Is the poor, weak zebra which is about to be pounced on.

The second sorrow of the lion,
Is the gunshot of the hunters,
Where we say goodbye to our lion friend.

The third sorrow of the lion,
Is the cry of the lioness,
Because of the loss of her cub.

The fourth sorrow of the lion,
Is the tired lioness after doing all the work,
Whilst the male lion watches her.

The fifth and final sorrow of the lion,
Is the cry of the circus lion,
Encaged for life.

Joe Bolton (10)
St Christopher's Catholic Primary School, Codsall

The Cool Car

A car is like a human,
But without the 7 life processes.

When you are at the traffic lights,
The engine purrs, talking to you,
Especially if it has a well-tuned exhaust fitted.

When you press your foot on the pedals
The engine makes the car go as fast as a cheetah
Leaving a trail faster than the wind.

When you want to stop
You put your foot on the brake
And the car screeches and screams
Leaving a trail of skid marks behind it.

When you have finished racing rapidly with the engine
Sizzling softly you park it outside your house
And leave its personality off
Trying to be human with its tyres to go to sleep.

Liam James Murrin (11)
St Christopher's Catholic Primary School, Codsall

Bored!

I am sitting in the classroom,
My brain thumping with my heart,
I am thinking of a poem,
But I don't know where to start!

With a happy or a funny,
The beginning of an end,
I am still thinking of a poem, but I really need to send . . .

It off for an audition,
To get it in a book,
I don't think they'll understand me,
Unless they really, really *look!*

I must put it in a postbox,
And send it far away,
Is a postbox spherical?
I don't care anyway!

So I am still thinking of a poem,
I don't know what to do,
Well I better hurry up,
'Cause I really need the loo!

Jessica Lilly Hammond (11)
St Christopher's Catholic Primary School, Codsall

When Things Come Alive!

The lock had a shiver,
The key had a cold -
It was too far for the school library to unfold!

The books gave a sneeze, as the dust blew away.
Comics craned over the toddling toy books.
However so quiet, so near
The only thing any book fears -
Is the horror of the crime books, peering and shouting wherever you go . . .

The library has secrets that had not been told,
The grey hairs of the library professors - lecturing
The love books, staring eye to eye with a grin on their cover!

The adventure books so rearing to go!
They swing round the lampshade and jump over the chairs!
The library is a madhouse! It's very sure to say.
However the library doors open -
So the madhouse will start another day!

Hannah Dibble (11)
St Christopher's Catholic Primary School, Codsall

In The Dark

Walking back from the garden centre,
With the talking tree,
Waving my arm so much I could have taken off,
But it was the tree ready to scoff whatever it could bite!

A taxi loomed into sight,
It said, 'Hello,' but the driver was not so friendly.
A squeak of the brakes at the traffic lights.
Red, yellow, green go, so off with the taxi as it went right.

A walk round the corner,
Past the sauna, down to the bus stop.
The deep red buses with their gleaming headlights,
I really think I'm going to pop.

No chance here, just fancy
Drivers, the guard dogs are let go,
Snap, snap, gnarl, grunt
I might as well take the scruffy, dirty bus.

Martha Bradbury (11)
St Christopher's Catholic Primary School, Codsall

A Recipe For A Fabulous Friendship

Firstly you will need a pot, but not just any pot; a banging pot!
So, fill your pot with water from a calm, clear river - a rippling sensation.
Add to your pot a cup full of sugar and education
Stir vigorously for 30 seconds.

To have a successful friendship you need to fall out,
So add to your pot the roar of a lion or the speed of a cheetah
Now a teaspoon of love plus a bubbling bowl of family.
Leave to simmer for an hour.

Now crack into a separate bowl, an egg full of golden opportunities
And a pint of food, water and health.
Put into the bowl a happy smile and a flower dancing about!
Now give it a whisk and add to your banging pot.

The final ingredient, the most important of all - quickly pour in a pint or
More of friends you trust, that will be there for life
Now slowly mix up and freeze until frozen
On a plate it goes, with its glowing friendly smile.

Orlagh Bonser (10)
St Christopher's Catholic Primary School, Codsall

The Memories Of The Old Victorian School

Walking down the path of the old Victorian school
Children walking the old stone staircase
The headmistress with a cane firmly in her hand
'Thirteen times one hundred and forty-two,' roared the teacher
Girls chatting, giggling and more
Boys playing tag, hiding behind gravestones
At the end of the day, in the old Victorian school
The children say their goodbyes
And run home with fear
With something in their eyes that looked like a tear
Those are the memories of the old Victorian school.

Alicia Burke (10)
St Michael's CE Primary School, Lichfield

Killer Kitchens!

Are you ever scared, of something very ordinary?
I'm afraid of the kitchen and all that is within!

The tormenting toaster terrifies,
With its bread-consuming eyes.

Oh I'm afraid of the kitchen and all that is within.

The microwave mischievously melts
Whatever falls inside its ring,
A certain death is assured when you hear its sudden *ping!*

I'm afraid of the kitchen and all that is within.

Watch out for the cruel cooker with its fiery heat,
Left without notice it may burn your meat!

Oh I'm afraid of the kitchen and all that is within!

Slippery and sly,
The sink knows not why,
It's water, hot or cold,
It may freeze or may scald.

I'm afraid of the kitchen and all that is within!

The blender, like a venus flytrap waits for a spider
To creep inside her.
And once on the blade . . .
Bbbrrrrrrrrr
Arachnid lemonade!

But I am afraid of a kitchen.

I know what you are thinking,
I must be dim of a kitchen and all that is within!

Abigail Kershaw (10)
St Michael's CE Primary School, Lichfield

Emyr

Emyr was a brave, young boy,
Who never said no!
He was my cousin and brought joy,
And a smile to every family I know.

Emyr had such great, great friends,
Who laughed and laughed all days!
But our memory of him never ends,
And up above the clouds he plays.

Dry those tears and do not cry,
We know he is still with us.
The cancer had to make him die,
We all sadly had to say goodbye.

His family and I had so much fun playing in the sun,
But this time passed us by leaving no traces of fun.
Down here now we sit and think,
Why did his spirit have to sink?

He wrote a book called 'Pigs in Space',
Which helped Latch too.
If everyone helped that would be the case,
Who would say they didn't care, oh who, oh who?

Eleri Van Block (10)
St Michael's CE Primary School, Lichfield

Sparky And Snow

At the top of my garden there is a shed,
And in there, there is a bed.
In that bed there's lots of hay,
And that is where my guinea pigs stay.

Snow's coat is white and smooth,
If you stroke her she'll never move.
In the dark she can hardly see,
But she sniffs around and knows it's me.

Sparky's fur is black, brown and white,
Her tufts stick up like she's had a fright.
This little pig is a drama queen,
She's like a squeaking jumping bean.

I take them their breakfast and their tea,
They're always looking out for me.
One is mad and one is bright,
But I will always love them day and night.

Nina Poley (10)
St Michael's CE Primary School, Lichfield

Shipwreck

The ghostly shipwreck drifted by,
Its sails high up in the black night sky.
It was a dark and cold stormy night.
When the tall ship sailed into sight.
Tossing the ship with all its power,
The wind grew stronger by the hour.
Even though the lighthouse foretold the dangers,
It was too late for those helpless strangers.
The furious waves flung the ship ashore,
What was once was no more.
And in a breath the sea was at rest,
The secret hidden beneath, no one would guess.
But the poor men on board lost their lives,
Never again to see their wives.
The ghostly shipwreck drifted by,
Its sails high up in the black night sky.

Charlotte Allerton-Price (11)
St Paul's CE Primary School, Stafford

Demon

I am running, running so fast,
I am running away from the demon.

With its bloodshot eyes
Fire within it
Death itself
It's the demon.

Spikes on its back
As sharp as knives
Nowhere near blunt
It's the demon.

Its fiery bright red body
Scaly and slithering across the ground
It's the demon.

Horns on its head
Deadly but true
Bashing everything in its way,
It's the demon.

Its teeth as black as a witch's cat
In the night sky eating everything
It's the demon.

Its growl as loud as thunder and lightning
It's the demon.

Its ears listening out all the time
It's the demon.

It follows me everywhere I go
Never leaving me alone,
It's the demon.

Harrison Smith (10)
St Paul's CE Primary School, Stafford

Seasons!

Cold, damp weather, rain around.
Colourful leaves fall from trees.
My favourite time
Autumn.

Warm and hot sun,
Beaches galore
Sand in my toe
Best time of all
Summer.

Daisies and daffodils spring and jump,
Soft petal flowers and animals race.
Amazing
Spring.

Cold snow, hot cocoa
Best addition to a night
So special
Winter.

Colourful, damp, snowy,
I love the seasons.

Ethan Crompton-Jones (11)
St Paul's CE Primary School, Stafford

Silent Shore

As I walked along the deserted beach,
The grainy sand tickled my feet.
The sea was a bright blanket of blue.
I saw a seagull but away it flew.

My nose crinkled because of the breeze,
Goosebumps appeared on my knees.
The horizon sat still upon the sea,
But the waves were reaching out for me.

I wandered back towards my home,
Behind my back was a sea of foam.
Tomorrow I'll return once more,
To stand alone by the shore.

Natalie Brown (11)
St Paul's CE Primary School, Stafford

The Night And Daytime Seabed

The sea's salty, icy skirt
Splashes on hard stone rocks.
The sky is covered in a navy blanket.
The sparkly stars hang in the night-time sky
Like beautiful pearls lying on a soft bed.
The dusty clouds glide in the air
Like pink-coloured candyfloss.
The glowing moon smiles and says goodbye.

As a big ball of fire explodes from the sea's end
The sand was now soft and warm
Like tiny breadcrumbs.
The sea was now hot like hot chocolate filling a giant teacup.
The rocks were now slimy and all kinds of creatures came out to play.
Seagulls did glide in the sea-blue sky.
And when my mum calls I know it is time to go
I shall leave with my head full of all my memories
About my night and daytime seabed.

Olivia Eve Sproston (11)
St Paul's CE Primary School, Stafford

My Summer Break Is Here

The sun is like a cup of tea,
All the fish are as small as a pea,
Waves crash so smoothly,
My hair floats like in a movie,
My summer break is here!

Sand melts me down,
Under the soft ground,
Houses up high,
Stars twinkle in the sky,
My summer break is here!

Candy canes on the hill,
Chocolate fills the golden mill,
Creamy chocolates floating down,
Sugar sweets form a town,
My summer break is here!

Caitlin Samuel-Camps (9)
St Paul's CE Primary School, Stafford

Football

He shoots
He scores
He runs like mad
It's the greatest goal he ever had.

An hour later
When it starts to rain
The ball hits him
And he dies of pain.

At the final whistle
With one guy dead
The team had won
But cries instead.

At the funeral
It was very sad
But they all remembered
The greatest goal he ever had!

Andrew Turner (11)
St Paul's CE Primary School, Stafford

Coke

My dad likes Coke cos he's a bloke.
He likes lemonade,
He likes the song 'Grenade'.

My mum goes shopping
She goes super hopping
She cuts with a knife
She likes the 'Champagne Life'.

My dad likes Coke cos he's a bloke.
He likes lemonade
He likes the song 'Grenade'.

My brother likes Mr Bean
He likes being seen
He plays water polo
He likes 'Ridin' Solo'.

Joseph Glayshier (9)
St Paul's CE Primary School, Stafford

Swimming!

Swimming is fun, it really is!
First your hat, goggles, trunks, kitbag and drink
Get in the water, *splash, splash, splash!*
Out come the pull buoy, fins and kickboard
First we practise freestyle and backstroke
Then we train on breast stroke and butterfly
Coaches also teach us to dive off the blocks.

All this training prepares us for the galas
When we want to do our personal best
We compete to challenge our own times
And to win some medals for our club
There is lots of cheering from the spectators
And great support from the rest of the team
Racing is fun, it really is!

James Evans (10)
St Paul's CE Primary School, Stafford

I Went For A Walk

I woke up in the morning
I went downstairs
I found a baby wrestling my favourite chair.

I went to walk outside
And I found a giant toadstool
Going down my slide.

I was walking in the woods
And I found
Lots of pixies drinking lots of whiskey.

So if you ever go for a walk
You always see something strange
But you could be dreaming
But I definitely was not today!

Fergus Adderley (10)
St Paul's CE Primary School, Stafford

The Girl

She walks in the forest alone,
Kicking the leaves in front of her.
Her white face staring at you as you walk by,
She stares at you with her baby-blue eyes,
Tears run down her cheeks.
She walks there every day
Hoping for a friend.
Now she's put that behind her
And every time you see her she smiles at you
With her ruby-red lips and her blushing cheeks,
She's always skipping along the stony path.
You try to speak but you're too shy,
But then you go bright red
You've just had your first kiss.

Niamh Dale (10)
St Paul's CE Primary School, Stafford

Maths

Addition and subtraction
Is just my passion.
Multiplication and division
Is just a collision
Perimeters and area
Are so much scarier
Than shapes and angles
Which still get me in tangles
Teachers can be strict but
They know the tricks of mathematics.
Decimals and fractions
God that is a distraction.
Math has to be the best
But everyone hates it when it comes to the tests.

Emily Ferguson (11)
St Paul's CE Primary School, Stafford

Animals

I like dogs
I hate giraffes
I like cats
But I also hate rats.

Butterflies are pretty
Their patterns are titchy.

Moths are flicky and
Always in the light.

Flies are busy, busy, busy
Even in the night.

Keeping me awake
And giving me a fright.

Matthew Wright (10)
St Paul's CE Primary School, Stafford

Pets

My dog is the best
But he hates eating cress!
My dog is the best at
Beating school tests.

My pet snail and
It's slithering slimy tail.
My pet, the snail,
Loves eating the mail.

My cat is a bit fat!
My pet cat tries
To eat the house rat!

Lochlan Woolley (10)
St Paul's CE Primary School, Stafford

The Ghost

Crawling through the night,
Drifting through the crumbling wall.
Trees cracking their fingers as he passes by,
A shadow in the misty moonlight.

Scurrying feet sprint away when he comes near,
His shabby clothes lifeless on his bony body.
His body a shrunken form,
His blood-red eyes strike fear into everyone's heart
All alone in the dead world,
His past no one knows,
His future an endless path to nowhere.

Charlotte Cox (11)
St Paul's CE Primary School, Stafford

Music

There is pop,
There is rock,
There is rapping,
There is hip-hop,
There is jazz,
There is soft,
There is slow,
I just can't make
Up my mind
They all are
So great.

Emily Hanson (9)
St Paul's CE Primary School, Stafford

Snow And Frost

There is frost on the trees,
You don't see bees.
There is frost on the grass,
The red robins pass.
There is frost on the bush,
There is always a shopping rush.
The snowdrops falling,
The birds are calling,
This is winter!

Joel O'Connor (11)
St Paul's CE Primary School, Stafford

Egyptians

E is for Egypt
G is for gods
Y is for yellow sun
P is for pyramids
T is for tomb
I is for the inner coffin
A is for ancient
N is for River Nile
S is for scarab beetle.

Lewis Penny-Slinn (10)
St Paul's CE Primary School, Stafford

Hair

Hair, hair it's everywhere
It's black, it's grey, it's there all day
Unless you shave it off.
If you dye it red it will dye your head
If you dye it brown it will make you frown,
So keep your hair
And check if it's falling off.

Joshua Elliott (9)
St Paul's CE Primary School, Stafford

The Crazy Frog

There once was a crazy frog
Who went to Prague
So a robot
Said, 'What?'

So the robot
Went to dot
Some money
For his honey
But his honey
Didn't want it
So he had a bike to race
He went to say, 'You are ace
Do you want a race?'
So he said, 'That is ace . . . about the race.'

So they went to the four corners of the globe
On the road that they drove
They started when they departed

The race had started because they had departed
But the crazy frog does not know about the bomb

The robot has planted
So he ranted
On a planet by himself
On that shelf

But that crazy frog planted the bomb on his ride
But in pride
So he went *tick-tick, boom, boom*
To that robot
So he then went, *'Weeee!'*

Junia Jai Lawson (10)
Thursfield Primary School

Funland

This rhyme tells a story,
Of a world bathed in glory,
Where pencils were snakes,
And puddles were lakes!

And the rain was the sun,
And the sun was the rain,
And the wind was the thunder,
And over again!

And the cats all wore dresses,
And the dogs all wore boots,
And the pigs all wore skirts,
And the cows played the flute!

And chimps wore pyjamas,
And a dog with a beak,
Said, 'Bananas I seek!'
And jumped off a cliff peak!

And houses were chocolate,
And lamp posts were lollies,
And instead of cars,
They had shopping trolleys!

If you don't believe me
If you think it's too cool,
I can prove it to you
Just come to Thursfield School!

Aaron Oakes (10)
Thursfield Primary School

Matthew's Ear

There was a land in Matthew's ear
A place where no one would go near,
And in that land mushrooms could walk,
Not just that the pencils could talk,
They all ate jam every day,
'I like jam!' they'd all say,
The monkeys dance and prance and cheer,
That's all that goes on in Matthew's ear.

Katie Figgins (10)
Thursfield Primary School

The World Of Animals

A is for anteaters who eat ants
B is for bears who jump with a roar
C is for cats that scratch and snatch
D is for dogs that bark like a horn
E is for elephants that stomp like a giant
F is for frogs who are green and slimy
G is for gorillas who hit their chest
H is for hippos who live in a river
I is for iguanas who are dry and scaly
J is for jaguar who sprint through the jungle
K is for kangaroo that jumps for Australia
M is for monkey that hangs on trees
L is for leopard spots not stripes
N is for newt that glides in the pond
O is for octopus that blackens the ocean
P is for penguin that waddles in the Arctic
Q is for quail that lays eggs
R is for rabbit that burrows in the ground
S is for snake that slithers around
T is for turtle that owns the green
U is for unicorn that is a mythical creature
V is for vulture that flies through the sky
W is for whale who is a giant in the sea
X is for kisses xx to a koala bear
Y is for yak who are hairy with horns
Z is for zebra which catches the stripes.

Niamh Minton (11)
Thursfield Primary School

A Poem About A Thing

There once was a poem about a thing,
The thing would talk, the thing would kill,
The thing was very, very awkward.

There once was a poem about a thing,
The thing was lean, the thing was mean,
It's only a sprout with a snout.

Harrison Berry (10)
Thursfield Primary School

My High School Nightmare

I woke up in high school
But no one was there
The lights were all off
And the corridors bare

'Sorry my homework's late!'
I heard a boy bark
As the teacher put pen to paper
And began to mark

I had to find my classroom
I had to find it fast
As the teacher called the register
My name was first and last

The teacher called my name
Then gave me a devilish stare
I woke up all of a sudden
And my mum was standing there

'It was just a dream you silly fool
Now get up and ready
You've got high school.'

'Argh!'

Aimee Worth (10)
Thursfield Primary School

Stoke City FC

S upportive fans
T errible red cards
O wn players
K icking the balls in the net
E xcellent goal keeping

C racking goals
I mpressive noise
T errific hat tricks
Y ellow cards

F orever young
C ool, calm, collected.

Ronan Proud (11)
Thursfield Primary School

An Upside-Down World

Far away in a land of old,
Where trees were pink and clouds were gold.

Where the moon was green
And had no sheen.
Where the sun was blue
And the grass was too.

The caves were light
And gave no fright
But often the bats
Grew as big as cats.

Where hypnotist lollies
Danced their jollies
And all of the pigs
Worked on oil rigs.

A fearless pig
As big as a fig,
Jumped over a fountain
As tall as a mountain.

William Wilson (10)
Thursfield Primary School

Cake

I love cake
Especially the one Mum can make
I would sit all day to watch one bake

I sometimes take some to school
Everyone thinks I'm cool
But today I made myself a fool

Last night, I could not sleep
So I went downstairs to get a midnight feast
I opened the fridge and there was a cake
Mum would not mind in the least.
So I broke off a chunk and ate it like a hungry beast

It was not until the next morning to see how much I'd ate
I began to make up excuses but it was already too late.

Joe Booth (11)
Thursfield Primary School

Phill, The King-Eating Dragon

There once lived a dragon called Phill,
He lived in a cave in Brazil,
He once felt really ill.

He thought for a while then appeared a smile,
He was going to eat the King Kyle,
He walked for a while,
He got to the castle and said, 'Wow, I walked a mile!'

He got through the gate,
Gave the guard a great big smile,
And ate King Kyle straight.

The maid fell down,
As the dragon spat out the King's crown.

He then went home and gave out a groan,
Since the king hadn't turned off his phone.

Hannah Bourne (10)
Thursfield Primary School

Sweets

Twister, Twister make a sound
Twister, Twister turn around
Twister, Twister touch the ground

Curly Wurly, Curly Wurly, Curly Wurly stop
Curly Wurly, Curly Wurly, Curly Wurly hop
Curly Wurly, Curly Wurly, Curly Wurly pop

Ice cream, ice cream cherry on top
Ice cream, ice cream makes you go pop
Ice cream, ice cream when will it stop?

Mint, mint sitting on my shelf
Mint, mint all by itself
It's all mine!

Charlotte Heath (10)
Thursfield Primary School

Sweets Are Taking Over

Marshmallows, marshmallows pink and white,
Marshmallows, marshmallows they're so nice,
Marshmallows, marshmallows can't you see?
Marshmallows, marshmallows they're all for me.

Haribo, Haribo, in a mixture
Haribo, Haribo better than a picture
Haribo, Haribo it's so clear
Haribo, Haribo they're so near.

Jelly Tots, Jelly Tots everywhere
Jelly Tots, Jelly Tots in the air
Jelly Tots, Jelly Tots if you dare
Jelly Tots, Jelly Tots they don't care.

Courtney Gidman (10)
Thursfield Primary School

Freddo, The Frog

Freddo the frog is tall and straight
When he hops around the gate
Freddo the frog likes flies
But if he doesn't catch anything he cries.

Freddo the frog does a rap
With a bap and a cap
Freddo the frog likes to sing,
And he gave his wife a ring.

Hip, hop, hippity, hop
Hip, hop, hippity, hop
Hip, hop, hippity, hop
Hip, hop, hippity, hop.

Callum Pugh (11)
Thursfield Primary School

Colours

Red is a raspberry all juicy and sweet
Orange is an apricot which I can't eat
Yellow is the sun which sends out lots of heat
Green is the grass I like to run on in bare feet
Blue is the sky which is endlessly high
White is a cloud floating through the sky
Black is a hole where if you fall down you'll be saying goodbye
Pink is a pig, it smells so bad, it could make you cry
Brown is a puddle which is mostly mud
Purple are grapes which taste very good
Gold is a star which no one can reach but everyone wishes they could.

Lauren Kelly (10)
Thursfield Primary School

The Travelling Fish

Once upon a time, in a story of old,
A travelling fish,
Lay on feathers of gold.

Its name was Trish,
What a weird name
Wow, what an odd fish.

This strange little fish,
It travels, it talks,
But strangest of all, its name is Trish.

Elleanor Cornes (10)
Thursfield Primary School

Smithy - James Corden

Smithy, well what can you say?
Happy as can be in every way
Always there to lighten up your day
Full of charm, full of glee
Always there for you and me
Makes us laugh at the old TV.

Lucie Williams (11)
Thursfield Primary School

SpongeBob SquarePants

SpongeBob lives under the sea,
And that's good enough for me,
He loves to dance,
In his square pants,
He's always on my telly,
I watch him with a bowl of jelly.

Matthew Walker (10)
Thursfield Primary School

The Cheese

The cheese sat on a ledge
He was cut into a small wedge
The cheese grew legs
And started to begin a pledge
'I will promise you that I, Mr Cheese . . . Argh!'
Mr Cheese was blended!

James Fish (11)
Thursfield Primary School

The Boat

My heart is the engine, pumping away,
The windows are my eyes, looking one way.
My passengers are organs, keeping me moving,
The driver is my brain, taking me places.

My propellers are my legs, racing along the water,
The horn is my voice, a unique sound.
My structure is my skin, keeping everything in,
The fuel is my food, that keeps me going.

My heating is my breath, warm and cosy,
The lifeboats are my children, there to call on.
The hull is my bones, keeping me standing,
My bow is my nose, sharp and pointy.

Brendon Youlden (11)
Two Gates CP School

Lonely Window

Silently sitting,
Dark clouds gathering overhead
Helplessly sitting
Rain lashes my face
Thunder crackled in the air
Water spitting down on my window sill
Silence echoes all around.

Clouds passing over,
Sun smiled on
Rain clearing up
Seeing people
My happiness starts.

Sun coming all the way out
Sun smiling down on my window sill
My day is ending, sunlight passing
Moon started to come
Sun going in.

Moon is out,
It is dark, lonely,
Nothing to see,
Clouds overhead
Rain lashes my face
Thunder missing me
That is my window.

Macauley Bancroft (10)
Two Gates CP School

Fast As Lightning!

Zoom, zoom, there goes the racing car
Like it just spoke to me,
Fast as lightning there it goes,
All was left was smiling tyre marks.

Zoom, zoom, here it comes again
'Oh no, it's stopping to talk to me,'
The racing, red number 1 strikes again,
Hooray number one has won again.

Jake Robbins (10)
Two Gates CP School

The Window Of War!

I see Germans dropping bombs,
I see children singing songs,
I am the window of war,

I smell gas filling the air,
I hear sirens everywhere,
I am the window of war,

I see bombs falling down,
I see dark demons destroying the town,
I am the window of war,

I see children sobbing goodbye,
I hear Mother starting to cry,
I am the window of war,

I see Mother rationing food,
I hear children's delicate mood,
I am the window of war,

I see the bomb above falling down,
I am the window that cannot be found,
I was the window of war.

Danielle Woodhouse (10)
Two Gates CP School

The Lonely Window

I jump into my snow-white frame,
Looking, looking at the tree dancing effortlessly,
I try to speak to my neighbour
But they just exclude me.
How do you think I feel?

Children look through me out, not at me,
I am a transparent child,
I defend the children with my life,
I can see cars speeding past,
I am the lonely window.

Kyle Turner (10)
Two Gates CP School

No One Notices

I watch people go by
They see me sitting here
With a bold, basic, base
No one notices.

The raindrops are my tears
I cry when I get hit
I feel isolated sometimes
No one notices.

Bang! The door opens
The people look at me
Like I am a toy
That's just me, I'm a window
No one notices.

The birds tweet enchantingly
The trees move side to side
I am as still as a statue
No one notices . . .

Chelsea-Jade Beale (10)
Two Gates CP School

The Bike . . .

My feet are the working wheels with rubber soles,
My legs are the pedals turning along as I go,
My blood is the chain flowing around my body,
My skeleton is the frame so hard and sturdy,
My bum is my seat so soft and squishy,
My eyes are the lights shining so bright,
My arms are the handlebar grips sticking out strong,
My noisy nose is my horn honking along,
My mouth is the handlebars smiling at you!

For I am the bike!

Emily Broadfield (10)
Two Gates CP School

The Window Of Pane

The window sees everything
Except a World War
Screech goes the siren
I am the window of Pane

Shatter goes the other windows
I am lucky
Not the child in the room
I feel so sad
I am the window of Pane

I see the devastated streets
The worried women's faces make me shed a tear
The courageous children sneak into school
I am the window of Pane

The war has ended
England are victorious
I am still alive
I don't feel window Pane.

Sam Dean (10)
Two Gates CP School

The Emotional Window

I sit here all day and night
It gets boring stuck in a frame
I am the window of the hall

As the bell goes and the children flood the corridor
The children thump me with their shoulders
I am the window of the hall

As the children wash away my worst nemesis . . .
The thunder and rain punch me.
I am the window of the hall.

Morgan Walker (10)
Two Gates CP School

Maddie's Workshop

Featured Author:

Maddie Stewart

Maddie is a children's writer, poet and author who currently lives in Coney Island, Northern Ireland.

Maddie has 5 published children's books, 'Cinders', 'Hal's Sleepover', 'Bertie Rooster', 'Peg' and 'Clever Daddy'. Maddie uses her own unpublished work to provide entertaining, interactive poems and rhyming stories for use in her workshops with children when she visits schools, libraries, arts centres and book festivals. Favourites are 'Silly Billy, Auntie Millie' and 'I'm a Cool, Cool Kid'. Maddie works throughout Ireland from her home in County Down. She is also happy to work from a variety of bases in England. She has friends and family, with whom she regularly stays, in Leicester, Bedford, London and Ashford (Kent). Maddie's workshops are aimed at 5-11-year-olds. Check out Maddie's website for all her latest news and free poetry resources **www.maddiestewart.com**.

Read on to pick up some fab writing tips!

Nonsense Workshop

If you find silliness fun, you will love nonsense poems. Nonsense poems might describe silly things, or people, or situations, or, any combination of the three.

For example:

When I got out of bed today,
both my arms had run away.
I sent my feet to fetch them back.
When they came back, toe in hand
I realised what they had planned.
They'd made the breakfast I love most,
buttered spider's eggs on toast.

**One way to find out if you enjoy nonsense poems
is to start with familiar nursery rhymes.
Ask your teacher to read them out,
putting in the names of some children in your class.**

Like this: Troy and Jill went up the hill
to fetch a pail of water.
Troy fell down
and broke his crown
and Jill came tumbling after.

If anyone is upset at the idea of using their name, then don't use it.

Did you find this fun?

Maddie's Workshop

**Now try changing a nursery rhyme.
Keep the rhythm and the rhyme style, but invent a silly situation.**

Like this: Hickory Dickory Dare
a pig flew up in the air.
The clouds above
gave him a shove
Hickory Dickory Dare.

Or this: Little Miss Mabel
sat at her table
eating a strawberry pie
but a big, hairy beast
stole her strawberry feast
and made poor little Mabel cry.

How does your rhyme sound if you put your own name in it?

**Another idea for nonsense poems is to pretend letters are people
and have them do silly things.**

For example:
| Mrs A | Mrs B | Mrs C |
| Lost her way | Dropped a pea | Ate a tree |

**To make your own 'Silly People Poem', think of a word to use.
To show you an example, I will choose the word 'silly'.
Write your word vertically down the left hand side of your page.
Then write down some words which rhyme
with the sound of each letter.**

S mess, dress, Bess, chess, cress
I eye, bye, sky, guy, pie, sky
L sell, bell, shell, tell, swell, well
L " " " " " " (" means the same as written above)
Y (the same words as those rhyming with I)

Use your rhyming word lists to help you make up your poem.

Mrs S made a mess
Mrs I ate a pie
Mrs L rang a bell
Mrs L broke a shell
Mrs Y said 'Bye-bye.'

**You might even make a 'Silly Alphabet' by using
all the letters of the alphabet.**

**It is hard to find rhyming words for all the letters.
H, X and W are letters which are hard to match with rhyming words.
I'll give you some I've thought of:**

H - cage, stage, wage (close but not perfect)
X - flex, specs, complex, Middlesex
W - trouble you, chicken coop, bubble zoo

**However, with nonsense poems, you can use nonsense words.
You can make up your own words.**

**To start making up nonsense words you could
try mixing dictionary words together.
Let's make up some nonsense animals.**

Make two lists of animals. (You can include birds and fish as well.)

Your lists can be as long as you like. These are lists I made:

elephant	kangaroo
tiger	penguin
lizard	octopus
monkey	chicken

**Now use the start of an animal on one list and substitute
it for the start of an animal from your other list.**

I might use the start of oct/opus ... oct and substitute it for the end of l/izard
to give me a new nonsense animal ... an octizard.
I might swap the start of monk/ey ... monk with the end of kang/aroo
To give me another new nonsense animal ... a monkaroo.

What might a monkaroo look like? What might it eat?

**You could try mixing some food words in the same way,
to make up nonsense foods.**

cabbage	potatoes
lettuce	parsley
bacon	crisps

**Cribbage, bacley, and lettatoes are some nonsense foods
made up from my lists.**

Let's see if I can make a nonsense poem about my monkaroo.

Maddie's Workshop

My monkaroo loves bacley.
He'll eat lettatoes too
But his favourite food is cribbage
Especially if it's blue.

Would you like to try and make up your own nonsense poem?

**Nonsense words don't have to be a combination of dictionary words.
They can be completely 'made up'.
You can use nonsense words to write nonsense sonnets,
or list poems or any type of poem you like.**

Here is a poem full of nonsense words:

I melly micked a turdle
and flecked a pendril's tum.
I plotineyed a shugat
and dracked a pipin's plum.

Ask your teacher to read it putting in some children's names instead of the first I, and he or she instead of the second I.

Did that sound funny?

You might think that nonsense poems are just silly and not for the serious poet. However poets tend to love language. Making up your own words is a natural part of enjoying words and sounds and how they fit together. Many poets love the freedom nonsense poems give them. Lots and lots of very famous poets have written nonsense poems. I'll name some: **Edward Lear**, **Roger McGough**, **Lewis Carroll**, **Jack Prelutsky** and **Nick Toczek**. Can you or your teacher think of any more? For help with a class nonsense poem or to find more nonsense nursery rhymes look on my website, **www.maddiestewart.com**. Have fun! Maddie Stewart.

Poetry Techniques

Here is a selection of poetry techniques with examples

Metaphors & Similes

A *metaphor* is when you describe your subject *as* something else, for example:
'Winter is a cruel master leaving the servants in a bleak wilderness'
whereas a *simile* describes your subject *like* something else i.e.
'His blue eyes are like ice-cold puddles' or 'The flames flickered like eyelashes'.

Personification

This is to simply give a personality to something that is not human, for example 'Fear spreads her uneasiness around' or 'Summer casts down her warm sunrays'.

Imagery

To use words to create mental pictures of what you are trying to convey, your poem should awaken the senses and make the reader feel like they are in that poetic scene …
'The sky was streaked with pink and red as shadows cast across the once-golden sand'.
'The sea gently lapped the shore as the palm trees rustled softly in the evening breeze'.

Assonance & Alliteration

Alliteration uses a repeated constant sound and this effect can be quite striking:
'Smash, slippery snake slithered sideways'.
Assonance repeats a significant vowel or vowel sound to create an impact:
'The pool looked cool'.

Poetry Techniques

Repetition

By repeating a significant word the echo effect can be a very powerful way of enhancing an emotion or point your poem is putting across.
'The blows rained down, down,
Never ceasing,
Never caring
About the pain,
The pain'.

Onomatopoeia

This simply means you use words that sound like the noise you are describing, for example 'The rain *pattered* on the window' or 'The tin can *clattered* up the alley'.

Rhythm & Metre

The *rhythm* of a poem means 'the beat', the sense of movement you create. The placing of punctuation and the use of syllables affect the *rhythm* of the poem. If your intention is to have your poem read slowly, use double, triple or larger syllables and punctuate more often, where as if you want to have a fast-paced read use single syllables, less punctuation and shorter sentences.
If you have a regular rhythm throughout your poem this is known as *metre*.

Enjambment

This means you don't use punctuation at the end of your line, you simply let the line flow on to the next one. It is commonly used and is a good word to drop into your homework!

Tone & Lyric

The poet's intention is expressed through their *tone*. You may feel happiness, anger, confusion, loathing or admiration for your poetic subject. Are you criticising or praising? How you feel about your topic will affect your choice of words and therefore your *tone*. For example 'I *loved* her', 'I *cared* for her', 'I *liked* her'.
If you write the poem from a personal view or experience this is referred to as a *lyrical* poem. A good example of a lyrical poem is Seamus Heaney's 'Mid-term Break' or any sonnet!

All About Shakespeare

Try this fun quiz with your family, friends or even in class!

1. Where was Shakespeare born?

....

2. Mercutio is a character in which Shakepeare play?

....

3. Which monarch was said to be 'quite a fan' of his work?

....

4. How old was he when he married?

....

5. What is the name of the last and 'only original' play he wrote?

....

6. What are the names of King Lear's three daughters?

....

7. Who is Anne Hathaway?

....

All About Shakespeare

8. Which city is the play 'Othello' set in?

....

9. Can you name 2 of Shakespeare's 17 comedies?

....

10. 'This day is call'd the feast of Crispian: He that outlives this day, and comes safe home, Will stand a tip-toe when this day is nam'd, and rouse him at the name of Crispian' is a quote from which play?

....

11. Leonardo DiCaprio played Romeo in the modern day film version of Romeo and Juliet. Who played Juliet in the movie?

....

12. Three witches famously appear in which play?

....

13. Which famous Shakespearean character is Eric in the image to the left?

....

14. What was Shakespeare's favourite poetic form?

....

Answers are printed on the last page of the book, good luck!

If you would rather try the quiz online,
you can do so at www.youngwriters.co.uk.

Poetry Activity

Word Soup

To help you write a poem, or even a story, on any theme, you should create word soup!

If you have a theme or subject for your poem, base your word soup on it. If not, don't worry, the word soup will help you find a theme.

To start your word soup you need ingredients:

- Nouns (names of people, places, objects, feelings, i.e. Mum, Paris, house, anger)
- Colours
- Verbs ('doing words', i.e. kicking, laughing, running, falling, smiling)
- Adjectives (words that describe nouns, i.e. tall, hairy, hollow, smelly, angelic)

We suggest at least 5 of each from the above list, this will make sure your word soup has plenty of choice. Now, if you have already been given a theme or title for your poem, base your ingredients on this. If you have no idea what to write about, write down whatever you like, or ask a teacher or family member to give you a theme to write about.

Poetry Activity

Making Word Soup

Next, you'll need a sheet of paper.
Cut it into at least 20 pieces. Make sure the pieces are big enough to write your ingredients on, one ingredient on each piece of paper.
Write your ingredients on the pieces of paper.
Shuffle the pieces of paper and put them all in a box or bowl
- something you can pick the paper out of without looking at the words.
Pick out 5 words to start and use them to write your poem!

Example:

Our theme is winter. Our ingredients are:
- Nouns: snowflake, Santa, hat, Christmas, snowman.
- Colours: blue, white, green, orange, red.
- Verbs: ice-skating, playing, laughing, smiling, wrapping.
- Adjectives: cold, tall, fast, crunchy, sparkly.

**Our word soup gave us these 5 words:
snowman, red, cold, hat, fast and our poem goes like this:**

It's a *cold* winter's day,
My nose and cheeks are *red*
As I'm outside, building my *snowman*,
I add a *hat* and a carrot nose to finish,
I hope he doesn't melt too *fast*!

**Tip: add more ingredients to your word soup
and see how many different poems you can write!**

**Tip: if you're finding it hard to write a poem with
the words you've picked, swap a word with another one!**

**Tip: try adding poem styles and techniques,
such as assonance or haiku to your soup for an added challenge!**

Young Writers Information

We hope you have enjoyed reading this book - and that you will continue to enjoy it in the coming years.

If you like reading and writing poetry drop us a line, or give us a call, and we'll send you a free information pack.

Alternatively, if you would like to order further copies of this book or any of our other titles, then please give us a call or log onto our website at www.youngwriters.co.uk.

Young Writers Information
Remus House
Coltsfoot Drive
Peterborough
PE2 9BF
Tel: (01733) 890066
Fax: (01733) 313524

Email: info@youngwriters.co.uk

Shakespeare Quiz Answers

1. Stratford-upon-Avon 2. Romeo and Juliet 3. James I 4. 18 5. The Tempest 6. Regan, Cordelia and Goneril 7. His wife 8. Venice 9. All's Well That Ends Well, As You Like It, The Comedy of Errors, Cymbeline, Love's Labour's Lost, Measure for Measure, The Merchant of Venice, The Merry Wives of Windsor, A Midsummer Night's Dream, Much Ado About Nothing, Pericles - Prince of Tyre, The Taming of the Shrew, The Tempest, Twelfth Night, The Two Gentlemen of Verona, Troilus & Cressida, The Winter's Tale 10. Henry V 11. Claire Danes 12. Macbeth 13. Hamlet 14. Sonnet